MY LIFE IN BROADCASTING

It's been a lot of fun

MY LIFE IN BROADCASTING

It's been a lot of fun

CLIFF PEEL

Your Biography

First published 2016
Copyright © Cliff Peel 2016

All rights reserved. No part of this book may be reproduced or transmitted in any form or by any means, electronic or mechanical, including photocopying, recording or by any information storage and retrieval system, without prior permission in writing from the publisher.

Published in Australia by:
Your Biography
East Malvern, 3145, Australia
www.yourbiography.com.au
yourbiography@optusnet.com.au
Biographer: Gillian Ednie
Edited and produced by Ev Beissbarth

A Cataloguing-in-Publication record is available
from the National Library of Australia

ISBN: 9780646953854

Further copies of this book can be purchased at www.bookstore.bookpod.com.au
This book is available as an e-book from most major on-line bookstores
Typesetting and design by BookPOD
Printed in Australia by BookPOD
www.bookpod.com.au

Contents

Acknowledgements	vii
Preface	ix
1 Family history and early life	1
2 School days	9
3 Life on the farm	21
4 Starting work	33
5 Regional radio days	39
6 ABV2 TV Melbourne	67
7 Around the world in nine months	85
8 The tape age – TV and radio	105
9 The computer age	137
10 Retirement and even more fun!	145
11 Reflections	173

Acknowledgements

I am dedicating this book to the memory of my parents Lynn and Charles Peel. Gently but firmly, they nurtured my abilities, and gave me the education and guidance to allow me to take an interesting, exciting and adventurous path through life.

This book is dedicated equally to my life partner Rob Young who has given me love, support and companionship since we first met in 1971.

I wish to acknowledge the work of my biographer, Gillian Ednie, who has put my life story into a coherent form from my recorded ramblings.

My gratitude also goes to Ev Beissbarth, book editor and producer, who with due diligence has the book appearing as you see it.

A word of thanks to friends and colleagues who added their thoughts to this life story.

Cliff Peel
April 2016

Cliff as a toddler, at the farm gate

Preface

From a young age I've always been curious about the world around me. I've followed the trail in front of me whichever way it twisted and turned. That trail has led me from beginning my life on the farm, to the ABC news desk and finally all over the world. From childhood I've loved stamps and the places on them, and then as an adult I travelled the world to see those places. In my working life, I've been part of the transformation of broadcasting from Morse code and telegrams to the digitised 24-hour news cycle. I've always loved what I've done. I've been thoroughly blessed in the places I've worked, the countries I've visited, and the people I've met and shared my life with along the way. *My Life in Broadcasting – It's been a lot of fun* tells my story and I hope you enjoy reading it half as much as I've enjoyed living it!

Chapter One

FAMILY HISTORY AND EARLY LIFE

With one's life story there is always a beginning, and that for me was at 4.30 in the morning of Wednesday, 29 April 1936, in the reign of Edward VIII. So I am an Edwardian! The place was Kardinia House, a private hospital in Pakington Street, Newtown, a suburb of Geelong in south-east Victoria. Possibly the Chilwell and Newtown trams rattling by may have fostered my life-long interest in public transport – who can tell? I was a healthy baby, weighing 8 lb 4 oz (3.7 kg).

My parents, Lynn and Charles Peel, owned a mixed farm at Gnarwarre, some 20 kilometres west of Geelong at the end of the road that ran through the Barrabool Hills. It was literally the end of the road: one track went to our front gate, and petered

Cliff, about six months old, with mother Lynn

off shortly after into a gate which served the next-door property. The other track wound its way down the gully and past Mt Pollock to divide again into tracks going to Winchelsea and Inverleigh.

I was named Clifford Scott Peel. The Clifford came from Lieutenant John Clifford Peel, my father's far-sighted elder brother, who proposed the use of aeroplanes for what eventually became the Royal Flying Doctor Service. The Scott came from my mother's family name.

MY PEEL ANCESTORS

My great-grandparents on my father's side, George and Harriet Peel, were immigrants from Lincolnshire. They settled at Tower Hill, their property at Inverleigh, in 1856 after arriving at Point Henry near Geelong in 1852. My grandfather Charles Herbert was born at Tower Hill in 1871, the youngest of fifteen children, eight of whom survived infancy. He married Susan Everett, also at Inverleigh, and they had nine children. My father, Charles William, fifth in line, was born on 10 June 1904.

The Peel family home at Tower Hill, Inverleigh, built in 1856

My grandmother Susan Peel died in 1938 when I was only two years old. I don't remember her very well. My granddad Charles Peel died in 1966 when he was 95, so I do have good memories of him. He and my grandmother had ten children, John Clifford, George, Charles (my father), Robert, Tyrell, Jean and Arthur, and three others who didn't survive.

I never knew my uncle, John Clifford Peel, known as Clifford. He died eighteen years before I was born but I always knew his story. Clifford was a medical student when the First World War broke out and by 1916 he had joined the Melbourne University Rifles and the Citizen Military Forces. In 1917, he volunteered to join the newly formed Australian Flying Corps (No. 1 Special Draft), and was selected for pilot training at Point Cook. He was subsequently sent to England for further training and then on to the front line. Tragically, he lasted only a few weeks. Apparently, he was on a reconnaissance flight over northern France in September 1918 with John Patrick Jefferies, his photographer, and they have never been seen since. Obviously they were shot down somewhere, because there was no record of a landing or crash site anywhere. They just didn't make it back.

In November 1917, en route to England, Clifford wrote his famous letter to Reverend John Flynn, who was interested in creating a medical service for people in the outback. Flynn's idea was originally to use these modern newfangled motor cars. Peel said it would be

Cliff at fifteen months old, with father Charles

Lieutenant John Clifford 'Cliff' Peel in uniform

much cheaper and easier for a station to flatten out a 100-yard landing strip than to build a road over 100 miles, apart from the fact that planes were a lot quicker. On the second or third page of his letter, he outlined where the Flying Doctor bases should be, and practically every one of those is now a Flying Doctor base. John Flynn was a friend of my grandfather and would occasionally drop into the family home at Tower Hill in Inverleigh and I think that is where Clifford Peel got his interest. I've got a feeling that if he had finished his medical career, and got through the war, he would have been a brilliant flying doctor.

The Peel family celebrating the centenary of Tower Hill at Inverleigh, in March 1956

FAMILY HISTORY AND EARLY LIFE

THE SCOTT SIDE

On our mother's side, the history is not so well defined. I believe that my maternal great-grandparents, John Henry and Elizabeth Scott, came from northern England and settled in the Melbourne suburb of Surrey Hills in the 1850s or 1860s, about the same time as the Peels. Interestingly, the original family homes in both Inverleigh and Surrey Hills are still occupied by family members.

John Henry Scott, who came from England as a ship's carpenter, set up as a plumber in Union Road, Surrey Hills, right next to the railway crossing. One of his sons was my grandfather, Thomas Edward Scott, who married Ada Martin. Her parents (my great-grandparents) were William and Eliza Martin. William was always thought to have jumped ship in Melbourne, but was apparently put off the ship because he was so sick from the lack of fresh food on the voyage. Thomas was a fireman. The Scott family lived in Russell Street in Surrey Hills. Thomas and Ada Scott had eleven children, eight girls and three boys: Lily, Clara Evelyn Edith (my mother, Lynn, born 10 June 1901), Ruby, Hazel, William, Edward, Marjorie, Laura, Dorothy, Nancy and Garnett.

I don't recall much about my maternal grandparents, because my grandfather Thomas died when I was about four or five, and my grandmother Ada died a few years later in the late 1940s. She had Parkinson's disease and was always shaking. In those days, during the war, it was very hard to drive to Melbourne because of petrol shortages. Several times we went by train to visit my grandparents. We travelled in the red carriage in a non-smoking compartment and occasionally in the Ladies' section where toddlers were allowed. At night, the blackout rules meant that the shutters had to be down all the time and there were blackout strips across the headlights of the steam engine which therefore meant a slow journey.

I don't know too much about my parents' early life or how they met each other. At the time, Mum was a nurse at the Royal Children's Hospital which is not far away from Melbourne University where

Dad was training to be a Presbyterian minister. I presume that they met at a local dance or maybe at the University. Dad was living at Ormond College, and Mum did her nursing training and certificates in the Royal Women's Hospital and the Royal Children's Hospital, and was living in various Nurses' Homes nearby. They married in 1932 during the Depression. The best man was Clifford Auldist, Dad's good friend from theological college, and the bridesmaid was Mum's sister Hazel. I don't know why he changed his mind about being a minister and went into farming instead. I think the church was lucky and I think the farming community was lucky that he decided on farming because he was not a very good speaker. He was a good farmer though.

My parents married later in life than most people did at the time. Dad was 28 and Mum was 31. I was born in 1936 and my sister Lynnette was born in 1938. I rather hope she tells her own story. She, like me, started off at the Gnarwarre State School and from there she went on to Morongo Presbyterian Girls' College in Geelong. Lynnette attended the University of Melbourne where she completed a master's degree in agricultural science and later obtained a doctorate.

That is my background, so I'll call myself a 'dinkum Aussie' with European forebears.

Earliest memories

My memory of the first four years on our property Callemondah are fairly hazy: just a lot of animals, chooks, cows, sheep, and big vegetable garden with fruit trees, and Mum's smaller flower garden where she managed always to find enough flowers when it was her turn to decorate the little church we went to. The little church was the former state school at the place once called Laketown on the Princes Highway between Geelong and Winchelsea. Apparently it used to be a staging place for the coaches travelling between Geelong and Warrnambool and it was right near Lake Modewarre, hence the name. The school, church and hotel have all now long gone as has the nearby railway station at Buckley. I do remember that during the Second World War some of the young men of the area returned from the war and a large group of local people greeted the train as it ground to a halt at the tiny platform. To a small boy the fearsome black snorting locomotives were wonderful and frightening things to watch.

The Second World War was probably the first event I became aware of during those formative years with the family. We listened to the 12.30 pm and 7.00 pm news on 3AR, the ABC station that we regularly tuned into, and the local news from 3GL, which called itself the 'Geelong Advertiser' station. We had to black out our house because it was right on top of the hill overlooking the Barwon Valley. When Dad could find petrol he had to paint his headlights black with just a bar showing if he drove at night. Mum used to stand on the running board with a torch at times when the track was difficult to negotiate in wet weather. Because Dad was a farmer, he could get petrol coupons to get his produce from our farm into Geelong.

One time I remember Dad got a permit to drive from Geelong to Melbourne and had saved enough petrol coupons to buy the fuel. He later told me he was instructed not to stop between the air force bases at Werribee and Laverton and that, if the car broke down, he had to get out and wave the white flag. Otherwise, he was told not to stop in any circumstances and also that he could be used as a target by pilots training at the nearby Point Cook air base. I remember sitting between Mum and Dad in the 1936 Ford utility, our only means of transport, as one of the training aircraft made dives at our utility. There were very few vehicles on the Melbourne–Geelong Road at the time and this was a lucky break for the trainee pilots! I was petrified but Dad drove grimly on. I must have slept through the return trip.

The family property Callemondah, with Lynnette and Lynn on the right, 1957

Chapter Two

School days

Gnarwarre state school

I started school at the local primary school, Gnarwarre State School, in 1942. At the tender age of five, I rode the two and a half miles each way to school along a corrugated gravel road on a fixed wheel bicycle. I had no other way of getting there, except by walking. Lynette rode the pony and so we went our separate ways. I did have one advantage, though: when the cream man came along to collect from our farm, I could put my bike on the cream truck and get a lift to school which she couldn't do with her horse!

It was a one-teacher school with about twelve students that went all the way through to the end of primary school. During the time I was there, we had only one teacher,

Lynnette on her pony, circa *1944*

Robert Patrick Murphy. He was a retired naval officer who had got the job of teaching because, in 1942, there were not too many people around to teach in little one-man state schools, and mostly they were one-man in those days. He used to come out from Geelong by train and get off at a little place called Murgheboluc which was about 10 kilometres from our school. On Monday mornings he would get off the early-morning mixed goods train, and walk the 10 kilometres including wading a ford on the Barwon River. It was about 11 or 12 kilometres to the bridge if the river was flooded and he couldn't get across. He stayed in a farming cottage during the week and then Friday afternoons, we finished school pretty punctually and he walked the 10 kilometres back to catch the evening train back to Geelong where he spent the weekend.

He was a pretty tough old bloke. Discipline was fairly good and he had a pretty good strap too which I experienced once or twice. I don't remember too much about my schooling except the teacher was excellent at maths and I think the strap helped us remember the times tables. And it did work later when I was doing night school, and working at Woolworth's as a 'counter jumper', I could multiply such sums as three and nine pence by five very quickly. I also liked being with a whole lot of other kids roughly my own age – it was great to get away from being on your own on the farm all the time.

LORNE AND LEARNING TO SURF

My father taught me how to swim at Lorne when I was about four or five, where my grandfather on Dad's side had a house that was purchased by Susan Peel in 1919. We went there every summer for two weeks during the holidays. In the 1940s, 1950s and 1960s, Lorne was a quiet little place, not at all built up. Dad taught me by hanging on to the back of my shorts while I floated in the water, and then showed me the strokes and how to move. I just picked it up as I went along, and soon felt quite confident in the water.

School days

My grandfather made surfboards out of redgum for the whole family to use, and we kept them in the bathing box on the beach. Those boards weighed a ton, and weren't curved or anything like that. They were just huge flat boards. You couldn't stand up on them; that design came in later. I had a smaller board because I was not big enough to handle the full size. Even so, the board was 1½–2 metres tall, taller than I was! All the kids had the use of the boards, and my father taught us how to body surf as well as surf on the boards.

The board was hard to manage, and sometimes I didn't manage it well – if I got a wave slightly the wrong way, the board would fly up, and I'd go down. So as soon as that happened, I'd just hit the bottom of the sea, and wait for the board to go up in the water above me. Also I had to make sure the board wasn't in front of me, because if I fell off the board, the board would go with the wave. It was really dangerous. I would swim this big, heavy board out, more or less under the water, and then try to catch a nice wave back in to shore. In those days you weren't tied to the board, so if you fell off, you'd just have to swim to retrieve it.

Dad could manage it really well. He'd go right at a good big wave, and come flying in, but he'd lie on the board – he wouldn't try to stand up. No one stood up. The idea was to get on top of the wave and really come right down with it. You had to keep the nose of the board up. And it was a real thrill.

In those days at Lorne, I used to surf with the family, sometimes just my sister, or by myself. It wasn't a surfing community like there is now. There was little or no professional surfing in the 1950s. Surfing really only began in Hawaii in the 1930s, and properly designed boards didn't exist until the 1960s or later. Surfing took off with the invention of fibreglass boards. Before that you needed to be extraordinarily strong. There was a surf lifesaving club at Lorne even in those early days, but I didn't join it since I was only there for a fortnight every summer. But I got a real taste for it from those holidays.

'Nardoo', the family's seaside retreat at 58 Smith Street, Lorne

Lynnette and Cliff, circa *1946*

Boarding at Geelong College

In 1946, straight after the war, my father decided it was time to for me to move on. I was sent off as a boarder to Geelong College when I was nine, nearly ten years old, and boarded there for eight years until 1953. In those days, there was no public transport, Geelong was 20 kilometres away, my parents couldn't afford to drive me there as petrol was still scarce, and it was too far to ride a bike so there was no other option. Lynnette later went to Morongo in Geelong. Eventually there was a bus but not in the early days.

I was one of the younger ones but there were some even younger – eight or nine years old – and again they were mainly from farming areas in the Western District. There were not too many options open for them to get their education and so, if parents could afford it, they put their sons into the College or they might also go the other school in Geelong, Geelong Grammar. Geelong College and Geelong Grammar were the two big boarding schools and there was Morongo and The Hermitage for the girls; now both former boys' schools are coeducational.

Cadets in kilts, Geelong College, circa *1948*

It was a strange environment, a very different environment to Gnarwarre State School where it was just local kids. In those days it was sort of very English style, lots of bullying, the way the teachers themselves behaved … the school was not in good condition because of the Second World War. There were no young people to teach us. A lot of teachers were well and truly nearing or over retirement age. New ones came in in the later 1940s and early 1950s.

Not surprisingly in an all-male boarding school, where egos are full blast, there was a clear pecking order based on bullying. It was the old natural animal thing, a bit like 'Lord of the Flies', with everyone trying to dominate the other. If you want to dominate, and you think the other bloke is weak, good, go for it! The school's view was clear: 'If you're bullied, don't go whinging to us, go and hit him back.' I did the same thing; if I saw a bloke who was weaker than me, I'd bully him. You had to be tough to survive and be prepared to look after yourself; you got a bloody nose occasionally and you gave a few. Dominance was also part of the competitive approach to sport. You were always encouraged to play sport, to be on top and to be in the top team.

In one way, it was a good way of being prepared for life, for the wide, wide world, when you don't have any protective people around to help if you're on your own. You learned how to look after yourself fairly quickly, and then you learnt to just watch out for the people coming up behind you, both students and teachers.

There was corporal punishment back in those days and everyone had a go at it. One teacher's favourite activity was walking around with his cane in his hand. If you were doing a good job you got patted lightly on the back; if you were doing a bad job, you got patted a bit harder further down. Even the prefects used the cane occasionally. They had the right to if they wanted to.

One of the things I discovered at school was the nature of my sexuality. There was no sex education whatsoever and I was more attracted to boys than girls and I thought this was completely natural.

I was in a boys' school and thought all the boys were like me which got me into a bit of trouble. I was probably saying things to boys that I shouldn't have said but I thought it was just a normal thing – no one told me any different. I was probably a bit effeminate and did have several nicknames that I won't repeat, but that was just part of the culture. However, I soon found out how I was different, and I did learn to fight. I stopped a lot of bullying once when I took on the biggest bully and said, 'I'll fight ya!' That brought half the school to a standstill to watch. After I hit him a couple of times, he decided it was all too hard and went home. That made a difference. In fact, I learnt to fight very early on. I remember crying to Dad while I was at state school, 'Someone hit me at school.' He said, 'Well, go and hit him back!' So I did and that worked!

Fortunately for me, I was not a small boy. I was quite tall, strong and well-fed – country 'bread and buttered' as they say. The food at Geelong College was 'nutritious' which was about the best way to put it. The menu was the same every week – you could never forget what day of the week it was. We had the roast on Sunday, cold meat on Monday, the shepherd's pie on Tuesday, chops on Wednesday, maybe sausages on Thursday and, being a good Presbyterian school, we had fish on Friday because it was cheaper on Fridays for the Catholics so we made sure we got some too. Then Saturday you were never quite sure what was going to turn up – whatever was cheap.

Sport, music and cadets

My most memorable time at school was when I was in Warrinn House, the house for 15- to 16-year-old boys doing their Intermediate Certificate.

There was an assistant housemaster and the matron, and the chaps in dark blazers were prefects; they were seniors and they stayed in the House as prefects to keep order (or attempt to keep order). I avoided trouble where possible. I was good at writing and I wrote a form newsletter once a month, encouraged by my English master,

Warrinn House, Geelong College, 1951. Cliff is fourth from right, second back row

until I got a bit libellous and was briefly banned from publishing. Eventually, all was forgiven.

As a school, we played football in winter. I couldn't play football very well but I could run so became a boundary umpire for the first eighteen. It wasn't too bad a job because we played football on Friday afternoon, as well as Saturday, so if I ran the boundary, I sometimes I got out of classes on Friday afternoon. It also included trips to Melbourne to Scotch College, Xavier College, Melbourne Grammar, Wesley and a few other places, so I had a bus trip thrown in as well. I loved umpiring later in life too and ended up briefly becoming a professional boundary umpire.

I also joined the rowing teams. At school you had to have a summer sport, that was either cricket or rowing, and having been hit a couple of times with cricket balls, I decided to take on rowing. We had a very good rowing coach and rowing club at the College. I progressed to the senior fourth eight and in 1952 we won the Head of the River. Our cox was a young, small chap called John Button, who ended up being Senator John Button. He was a very good cox and a very good prefect too. He coxed the first eight and they won the Head of the River the following year.

I always enjoyed the sea. We didn't have a swimming pool at Geelong College, so we used to go to swim at Eastern Beach, and even had swimming lessons there for boys who couldn't yet swim. We also swam in the Barwon River at Queen's Park, not far from the school.

In those days being in the cadets was compulsory, no getting out of it, that's why I joined the cadet band. I worked out that it was the easiest thing I could do. I had an E-flat bass (a tuba) which was the second largest instrument in the band. The beauty of it was that I could lug it around. You needed a certain amount of strength to be able to march up and down and carry the fool thing around. We had band practice two or three times a week – it was fun.

I also learnt music and the piano. I remember getting time off to practice. I was also a member of the Glee Club which produced a Gilbert and Sullivan school musical each year. We did *The Mikado*, *The Pirates of Penzance*, *HMS Pinafore*, *Iolanthe* and *The Gondoliers* and we had to follow the D'Oyly Carte copyright instructions.

Cliff aged 16, in the cadet uniform of the Gordon Highland tartan, with his E-flat bass

Actually, to get a whole lot of juvenile boys singing and taking part in the chorus in the 1950s was a pretty good achievement. I was in about four of them, I think: *The Gondoliers, Iolanthe, Pirates, HMS Pinafore*. Before my voice broke, I played a young girl in *The Pirates of Penzance*. I was one of the sisters, cousins or aunts, that sort of thing. When my voice broke when I was about 13 or 14, I remember playing the peer (a lord) in *Iolanthe*. I didn't play any major roles. I still love the music and have got most of them, including the D'Oyly Carte versions on CD.

In my last year at Geelong College, I experienced my first 'overseas' trip. During the May holidays in 1953 a classmate Barton Stott (now a retired County Court judge) and I hitchhiked around Tasmania. In those days most young people did not own cars and hitchhiking was quite common. Both sets of parents didn't appear too concerned about two 17-year-olds wandering on their own around the 'Apple Isle'.

We sailed from Melbourne on the *SS Narooma*, travelling overnight to Devonport from where we took the train (a diesel railcar) to Launceston. We stayed with the Presbyterian minister, the Rev. Clifford Auldist (the best man at my father's wedding) for a couple of days. We then hitchhiked to Hobart by way of the east coast and the Midlands to Hobart. We carried two one-man tents and camped out at night. From Hobart we hitchhiked to the Central Highlands, using our emergency money to stay overnight at Miena near the Great Lake as there was no suitable ground to pitch a tent. We ended our journey again at Devonport to take the *SS Taroona* back to Melbourne.

We had no trouble getting lifts from the few cars on the roads in those days and from the slow-moving H.E.C. (Hydro Electric Commission) trucks used in building power plants in the Central Highlands. It was my first taste of adventure tourism.

After passing my Leaving, I stayed on to do Matriculation but did a glorious failure on that. The school encouraged everyone to

Cliff with Barton Stott on board the SS Taroona, *May 1953*

matriculate, although in the 1950s you needed Matriculation only to enter university. Most pupils who had a career already worked out, which generally meant going back to their father's business or farm, would leave after they got their Leaving Certificate. I decided that I would go back and become a farm boy and work with my father on his farm. So that's where I went.

Chapter Three

LIFE ON THE FARM

Our farm was at Gnarwarre which is Aboriginal for parrot swamp – Gnar is parrot and warre is swamp and Modewarre, Gnarwarre, Connewarre are all swamps around Geelong. There are not many parrots there now, because in the 1940s and 1950s the swamp was drained to turn it into agricultural land. It gets wet occasionally but it is no longer a swamp.

The road to Callemondah with Mt Pollock in the background, December 1965

Ours was a mixed farm – we had about 600 hens, with all the egg washing that went with them, a few cows to milk, and we grew oats and barley. We also had sheep. We started with 600 acres which Dad doubled to 1200 when the opportunity came up. I think Dad was a very hard worker. Reckon I did my fair share of work as well! Mum was a very good organiser, and a fairly good disciplinarian. She kept me on the more or less straight and narrow, and called me, 'Scotty by name, Scotty by nature' if she thought I was being a bit temperamental. Mum was also very good with finance and managing money. She taught me a lot in that respect: about budgeting, not wasting money. Somehow she managed to put a little bit of money aside for this, that, and the other thing.

Grandad Peel had a big farm not far away, about 10 kilometres, at Tower Hill in Inverleigh where he grew up and my dad grew up, so we saw quite a bit of him. He was a strong man and known to keep his sons under his thumb but not his daughters-in-law. Granddad had a hearing aid, one of the old-fashioned hearing aids that had a volume control which he kept in his pocket. I remember one day, Mum was getting stuck into him over something or other, and Granddad turned the volume down so he couldn't hear her. Mum just leaned across, turned it up, and held it in position 'til she'd said what she had to say. He never did that to Mum again! It was one of the funniest things I'd ever seen.

Lynnette and Cliff with their father at Lorne, dressed for church, circa *1948*

My grandfather did spoil his grandchildren rotten. There was always a ten-shilling note for Christmas. Of course, in those days, in the 1940s and 1950s, that was a fair amount of money. We didn't get any pocket money or anything like that, but we'd come in to town once a week for shopping ... and we might get an ice-cream bought for us. Mum used to seize the ten shillings and put it in my savings account.

I learned a lot from my grandfather Peel. He was always showing me and his other grandchildren things to do on the farm. Every now and again, he kept pigs to slaughter for bacon and all that type of thing. I remember, as little tackers, myself and my cousin, we'd go round and watch Granddad kill the pig, and then butcher it. Then it was our job to get rid of the hair on the hide, then rub salt into it. We salted everything down, because there was no refrigeration. On the farm, I watched Dad kill sheep and later he showed me how to cut their throats, skin and butcher them, and cut them up for the house. Chooks also; Dad showed me how to wring their necks and pluck them, clean them, and get them ready for the house. I was never queasy about this; it was just a normal thing to kill them.

Grandpa Peel planting a tree at Tower Hill for the Peel family's centenary celebration, March 1956

We would always be plucking chooks and cleaning them. One Christmas Eve I remember, we got a frantic call from a friend of my father, the owner of the Four Kings Roadhouse at Anglesea. He said, 'I've got a bit of a problem. I have 37 people coming for Christmas dinner, and the chooks for dinner are now strewn across the Melbourne–Geelong Road. The truck has overturned after an accident and I haven't got anything to feed the guests!' Dad and I had to wait until dusk to catch 35 chooks, as by then they had settled down for the night. As these hens were bred for laying eggs, we had to make sure that they had a bit of meat on them. We spent the next hour or two catching, killing them and cleaning them. Then we drove on the back roads to Anglesea with the chooks, arriving there about midnight and having a bit of coffee before driving back the same way, dodging the kangaroos. By then it was Christmas Day and, of course, we had chook for Christmas dinner, as you do.

I had a rabbiting dog and did a lot of rabbiting, spending most of my school holidays digging them out of their burrows. It was a very good dog because it caught the rabbits by the neck and wrung their necks. In those days, hydatids was a very, very serious disease which you got from farm dogs, and it was prevalent in the Western District. So we had to be very careful not to be licked and had to wash our hands if we were accidently licked. We shot and killed rabbits in any way we could, and ate them of course. Mum used to bake them, boil them, fry them, you name it. Basically, we lived off the land in those days, and luckily I loved rabbit.

I had a terrific sheep dog too. He was a Kelpie cross, mainly black but with white feet, so I called him Socks. I got him when he was about six months old, and he would work for me, but not for Dad. He was a one-man dog. Mum was good at hand-rearing the lambs whose mothers had died. They only stayed around until they were old enough to fend for themselves and join the flock. There were occasionally a few pet lambs that had to be bottle-fed. Mum would put the very weak lambs in front of the stove in the kitchen until they recovered. When they started to wander around, out they went! The vet was 20 kilometres away, on a gravel road, so only the most serious problems needed the vet. Occasionally, if a cow was sick, Dad would have to shoot it, and I know, though I had left home by then, that he had to shoot quite a lot of sheep that were burnt when a fire came through the property.

INVESTING IN THE FARM

Dad had gone into fine wool production, and wool was earning a premium. So the money was coming in. Farmers were willing to try new ideas. I remember he bought the first pick-up baler in the area. He went around the district with it, making money on that. We also had a rather fortunate experience, and God bless the Americans and their financial ability, or inability. The Korean War came along, and the American Air Force was bidding against the American Army for wool to make uniforms. That worked out well for us!

Dad never believed in paying income tax. He always spent money on the farm. He never did save very much money. I remember one year, he came inside and said, 'I've had to pay income tax.' He was quite upset that he had made so much money. He was always looking for innovations, and reinvested money into the farm after paying the bills. I remember we had the first Nuffield diesel tractor. We had a field day on our property, showing off this new tractor. It was a real powerful piece of machinery – in those days anyhow. Dad loved the farm; it was his hobby, his work, his farm.

THE DAILY ROUTINE

Life on the farm followed a fairly predictable pattern. We started by milking the cows, every day, twice a day, at six in the morning, came in for breakfast, and then worked until midday or quarter past twelve gathering eggs, cleaning eggs, and chasing sheep. Mum would cook a big two-course lunch (often chops or sausages with a dessert) and we would listen the twelve-thirty news and 'Blue Hills' at one

The farmyard at Callemondah, circa *1946*

o'clock. We went back to work until five or six o'clock and milked again before dinner, then back out again to lock up the chooks after dark. In the evening, I'd either go out somewhere, if I could, or stay home and listen to the radio, or after 1956, watch TV.

Social life

Like in all rural communities, social life revolved around the Country Women's Association activities and supporting the Red Cross for Mum, and the Volunteer Defence Force and Fire Brigade for Dad. As we grew up, we got involved in these things too. There was also the Presbyterian Youth Fellowship and the church. Despite Dad having begun to train for the Presbyterian ministry, he didn't talk much about religion. I think he worked on the theory that there was enough religion at boarding school to keep me going. In fact, he was a fairly quiet and uncommunicative person. Mum pretty much just went along with Dad; she wasn't very religious either but still went to church. It was a good place to meet people, and have a good gossip.

As I was the only son, I had to do the right thing; go back home and work on my father's farm after I left school. I did this for three years from 1954 to 1957. I joined the Geelong Young Farmers' Association which met about once a fortnight. I was also doing night school in wool classing. I did that for about two years. I was rarely home at night and Dad let me drive the utility which arrived on my eighteenth birthday. I had dreams of a Zephyr convertible, the car of the moment.

Lynn and Lynnette at Callemondah, 1957

Everyone joined the Rural Fire Brigade. We had CFA training once a month in Geelong and we also had some basic fire training on our farm. We had a six-tonne Bedford truck, and we could take two very large tanks of water on it. We also got, through the Fire Brigade, a pump and two hoses, and we could actually pump water from the tanks through the hose onto wherever it was needed. Dad had set up a very good water supply system on the farm using a huge dam he built in the late 1940s or early 1950s. He set up a windmill which filled a large tank on a big tank stand which used reticulated water

Stall run by Young Farmers' Club at the Geelong Gymkhana, 1955

Profile photo for On the Beach *audition, 1957*

to fill the water troughs for the sheep in those paddocks without waterholes. We could use this system to fill the two big water tanks in our Bedford truck within 10 minutes.

In 1957, there was bit of local excitement. The film *On the Beach* starring Ava Gardner was being made in Victoria and I applied to be an extra. I had to send a profile photo. They didn't choose me as an extra but I had friends who did get roles as extras.

Living in the country, sport was a big part of our social life. In summer, I played at the Barrabool Tennis Club, a little country club – not that I was ever a great tennis player. I think I made C grade, or something like that. I wouldn't put that down as a sporting achievement. It was a bit of fun on Saturday afternoons and if I didn't get away, Dad would have me working on the farm. I'd say, 'Look, I'm going off to play tennis.' He'd reply, 'Oh, that's all right then.'

Cliff, sporting a three-week beard after a camping trip to Mount Kosciusko, March 1957

Football umpiring

After I left school, I became a member of the Geelong Football Umpires' League. I did boundary umpiring, mainly because I could run. In fact, I was a boundary umpire in two District Grand Finals, and was awarded a Certificate of Merit for 'officiating as an umpire in a grand final match' in both 1956 and 1957.

In those days, they used Geelong umpires to provide boundary, goal and central umpires for the VFL reserve matches, or seconds match as it was called then, played at Kardinia Park prior to the main match which was umpired by a Melbourne umpire. Some of the best jobs I got were being the boundary umpire for the VFL seconds at Kardinia Park. Not only did I get well paid, two guineas per match which was quite a lot of money in those days, but I could sit down in front of the umpires' race and watch the main match; a real bonus there. We were also allowed to use the umpires' room before and after the matches. One of the umpires there that I can remember was Harry Beitzel, later famous for his football media career. It was great.

I did get booed by about ten thousand people at Kardinia Park once. It was the final quarter, and Geelong was behind by about two points. Somewhere in the forward area or half-forward area, one of the Geelong players took a brilliant mark. The only trouble was, he was over the line, right in front of the members' stand. I immediately blew my whistle, and there were ten thousand people who completely disagreed with my decision. However, you just had to ignore them.

Otherwise we would be boundary umpiring at little local matches in the Geelong area. Some of the country matches were quite fun too. I remember we had a grand final between St Mary's and Geelong West played at the Geelong West Oval. It was one of those terrible days when the wind was coming in straight from the Antarctic, and blowing into one pocket of the ground. The ball rarely moved out of that area apart from whenever there was a goal scored. It was a terrible game. There was only about two or three points in it. I think only about four or five goals were scored all round, or six goals. Anyhow, coming off there was a bit of a melee and the umpire, two goal umpires, and two boundaries all huddled together and went through this irate crowd, because of course the result was our fault! I remember one woman trying to push her husband in to hit the umpire; he was very reluctant, but he did knock the ball out of the umpire's hand. That was about the worst thing that happened that day. It was a bit frightening, but we got into the umpires' room eventually. At Geelong West the stand is built with good old-fashioned bluestone, with thick doors and bluestone walls, so we stayed in there, got changed, then poked our heads out for a look around. Everyone had found it all too hard and gone to the pub, so we went home.

There was no police presence at the football in those days. Anyhow, Geelong Football Umpires' League wrote to the police; or to the Association, and said we really need a police presence at some of these finals. Next week was one of those days and it was pouring rain. We were at East Geelong for a preliminary final. The police had taken notice of us and, as we went out on the ground in pouring rain, there were four policemen huddled together and about three spectators. I heard one policeman say to the umpire, 'Now, which spectator do you want us to look after?' We had to laugh at that. The vocal crowds were a lot of fun too. Occasionally, if you awarded a free kick, you would hear a lone voice roar across the ground, generally female, but sometimes male, 'You got the bloody rule wrong!' or words to that effect.

It was a lot of fun. The country people looked after the umpires very well, because they appreciated the fact that we made our way to the games in our own cars or whatever transport we could get, and we didn't get paid very much. They were just glad to see us so that their game could go on.

Deciding to leave the farm

In those days, farming didn't seem to be a career path and Dad didn't teach me very much. I did enjoy doing some PR work for the Young Farmers' Association in Geelong. In fact, I was President at one stage. The PR work involved being interviewed and doing some radio work for 3GL. While I was digging out thistles on the farm one day I thought it would be much more interesting to be on radio. So eventually, after I turned 21, I said, 'I'm off; I'm going to become a radio announcer.'

Dad didn't oppose me. We didn't talk about it at the time; we never talked very much. Dad was very much his own man, and he wanted to farm his own way. It was his farm, and on reflection, I think he was slightly relieved when I decided not to stay, because that meant he could stay and still have his farm, which was his hobby and his life. He more or less encouraged me to leave the farm. I think that was why Dad didn't carry on about my departure.

Fortunately, Dad was able to employ all the farm hands he needed. In those days, there were a number of country VFL players who weren't drafted or anything like that. The players were only part-time, and weren't paid much by the clubs, so they had to have jobs. Dad was member of the Geelong Football Club and had several Geelong football players working on the farm, including the two Lord brothers, Stewart and his identical twin brother Alistair, who won the Brownlow Medal in 1962.

Although there wasn't the aura around footy and footy players that there is today, football was important to us. As a member of Geelong, Dad had a seat in the members' stand, so he'd go in and watch the football. Occasionally I'd come home at weekends and we'd go in and sit in the stand and watch the game together.

Cliff and partner at the Senior Young Farmers' Club Dinner, Melbourne, 1957

Chapter Four

STARTING WORK

I had made the decision to leave the farm and, while I think this was basically a relief to my father, it was a big jump. Before I left town, Dad drove me in to see Reg Gray, the manager at 3GL, to get some advice. He listened to me do a voice recording, and then said, 'Well, Cliff, there's something about commercial radio – you have to have a voice that will *sell* things. That's what we have commercial radio for, to *sell* things, and unfortunately, with your voice, you'd have difficulty selling an ice cream in hell!' He told me that if I was really determined to have a career in radio, I could go to The Vincent School of Broadcasting. Bill Roberts was the principal then, and it was Bill who got me into radio work eventually.

The School was basically the training ground for young people going into commercial country radio. That's where you started off. You had to go through your apprenticeship in country radio before you got some big money in the city. A lot of famous broadcasters went through that school later: David Johnson and Brian Naylor, for instance.

THE VICTORIAN METER LABORATORY

The Vincent School had classes at night, which suited me because I needed to work during the day to keep myself and to pay the fees. I had seen an advertisement wanting a salesman for the Victorian Meter

Advertisement for The Vincent School of Broadcasting, February 1951

Laboratory. I didn't know anything about the equipment; all I knew was that the meters measured electricity in some form or other. That was the extent of my technical ability to describe what I was trying to sell! I started work there on 1 July 1957. Basically my job was to go around to as many companies as I could, introducing them to the fact that these meters existed, and trying to sell one to them.

I was a salesman, but because we didn't have a car, I had to get around on public transport to see the potential customers, and I learned a lot about Melbourne's transport system. In fact, to get to the Victorian Meter Laboratory I used to take the train from Middle Park, where I was living in a boarding house, then the train from the city to Footscray. Then I'd catch the tram in Ballarat Road to the corner of Maidstone Street, and walk a short way to the Laboratory. It used to take me about an hour each way.

At this stage I was going to classes at the Vincent School three nights a week. To get into the building, an old office block since demolished, you rang the bell, and a key would be lowered from a third-floor window on a fishing line. Once we had let ourselves in, the key would be retracted. The building also had very wide window ledges allowing people to move from room to room on the outside of the building during parties – I wasn't one of them. We had different courses; one was for actually being in front of a microphone and presenting, just reading copy and playing a record and things like that. Then there was a class in writing copy for advertisements. We were taught how to keep it short and snappy and within 30 seconds. We also had pronunciation classes in which you learned how to pronounce foreign languages by recognising the sounds even though you might not understand what you're talking about! It was a technique of looking at the words and then showing the correct way to pronounce it in that particular language. If you had something written in German, you could actually make it sound as though you knew something about the language. You would just look a word, divide it up into the sounds that you knew those letters made, and practice it a couple of times. You would just break it down gradually and then put it all together again.

I wasn't a great meter salesman – after four months I had not managed to sell one piece of equipment. The boss told me that

Boarding house in Middle Park, Cliff's window next to palm tree, February 1958

employing a salesman wasn't really as successful as the company had planned, and it might be a good idea if I looked around for something else (I wasn't sacked). I had already decided that wandering around on trams and buses all day wasn't much fun, so I took his advice. A week later, I started my next job, which was at Woolworth's in Bourke Street as a shop assistant and demonstrator salesman. I was grateful to my old maths teacher at school, who drilled us in times tables and mental arithmetic. There were no computerised tills. You rang the amount up and worked out the change in your head.

Spruiking for Woolworth's

Woolworth's was not keen to employ people over 21 just to sit down behind the counter and sell things; they had much younger and cheaper employees for that. I talked them into having a little display counter and spruiker at the entrance to the shop in Bourke Street (which is now Centrepoint). So then I spent about eight months selling everything from ladies' underwear to wind-up penguins and everything else in between – whatever happened to be special at the time. The idea was to draw people off the street and into the shop to start with, in the hope that they would stay in the shop to buy other things. It was fun.

One day, I was selling some 'beautiful' nylon ladies' panties for three and eleven pence a pair, 'at a bargain price for such beautiful, gentle, silken underwear'. A lady came in to the shop, grabbed a pair, and checked the size. I was just standing there, looking around at the crowd, when next thing, down go her old pants and up go her new ones! She handed me the old ones, which I gingerly wrapped up, and collected her three and eleven pence. The security girl said, 'Did you see what just happened?' I said, 'Yes, did you? Can you believe it?'

I was a better spruiker than I was a travelling salesman. In fact, one of the companies that supplied spruikers to various stores saw me and offered me a job, but I decided I wanted to stay with radio.

Woolworth's, Bourke Street, Melbourne, 1959

Not many people know that I was the Victorian yo-yo champion too, at one stage. The Woolworth's store manager, a person who originated from the Netherlands, said to me one day, 'Ah, Cliff, you are now a Victorian yo-yo champion. Here is your yo-yo.' I said, 'I don't know a thing about yo-yos!' His reply was, 'Here are some instructions. Go off and learn how to play. We are now selling yo-yos.' So I went away and spent two or three hours learning how to do one or two tricks. Then I had to stand on a platform, yo-yo in hand, performing those tricks. (When the tricks got too complicated, I dropped it.) We sold plenty of yo-yos, and when he came back that evening he said, 'You have done very well, we have sold £25 worth of yo-yos!' In those days that wasn't too bad a result. I had a lot of fun in that job at Woolworth's but I was never tempted to give up the idea of broadcasting to become a travelling yo-yo expert!

STRATHMORE THEATRICAL ARTS GROUP

Around this time I first got involved in theatre. The suggestion came from one of the other students at the Vincent School who was involved in his local theatre group. I was encouraged to do theatre to break down my reserve a bit, and so I also joined the Strathmore Theatrical Arts Group – STAG – in Strathmore, just past Essendon. Also I had a cousin, Dulcie (Peel) and her husband Rod Andrew who lived out that way, and occasionally I'd walk in there for a meal and a chat before rehearsals. I had known Dulcie and her family since we were children. Dad's brother, Uncle George, had an adjoining property so we were always visiting them or they us, or dipping our sheep there or some other farm-related activity. I remember my first role for STAG was playing Henry Bevan in *The Barretts of Wimpole Street* in April 1959.

THE CROWN LAW DEPARTMENT

I left Woolworth's in July 1958, and took up a job as a clerk in the Crown Law Department in early August. All I did was file documents relating to companies, court depositions and property matters. It was very straightforward – document A went into envelope A, that type of thing. It was a nice nine-to-five job from Monday to Friday; nothing notable. But because I was doing night school, it was ideal. I couldn't say that I was overworked at the Crown Law Department. Apart from filing, once a week I was sent to buy a whole lot of Tattersall's tickets for the Saturday draw for the staff, including the boss, and that was it. We didn't win a big prize – not while I was there anyhow.

The Crown Law Department was in Queen Street, and I could get a counter lunch for 1s 3d at the pub nearby. This was sausages and mash and veggies, and meals like that. It was convenient too because then I could go on to night school or theatre rehearsal straight after work.

The Vincent School of Broadcasting was actually designed and set up by the little country radio stations to provide them with people already trained, who could operate equipment, write copy and go on air. After two years of night school, I felt I was ready to be one of them. In April 1958, 2QN rang up the Vincent School and asked for someone who could write copy and go on air. Bill Roberts called me in and said, 'Cliff, I got a job for you. You are going to 2QN Deniliquin'. And so my career in radio began.

Chapter Five

REGIONAL RADIO DAYS

2QN DENILIQUIN

I was very busy at 2QN Deniliquin. It was my first job as a radio announcer in a small country commercial radio station, and, as expected, I did everything. The pay, I shall say, was not earth-shattering, but it was a fantastic learning experience. I wrote copy, I broadcast, I started up a little news service and I did other odd promotions and things like that. It was a great learning curve. I especially remember first thing in the morning following the instructions to turn the transmitter on ... Press button A, wait 5 seconds, press button B, wait 10 seconds, then about three or four buttons later, all in order, suddenly the station came on air.

There was only one weekly newspaper for the area but we provided a daily ten-minute news service. The station couldn't afford the cost of getting *The Age*, *The Sun*, or *The Argus* every day, so we had to create our own 'news feeds'. I used to lift news items from everywhere I could, including any one of the local district newspapers. I didn't have time to go out and do my own reporting. Occasionally people would phone in, or, if I was a bit short, I might phone the Town Clerk and ask, 'Do you have anything to tell us?' Of course, they liked using the local news service to promote the things they were doing. I might go along to the police station just across the road, and ask, 'Anything you want to tell us?' It wasn't in-depth reporting.

I wasn't the only one doing this, which made me laugh. One of the best items I found was a little filler that you could save and use any time when you were running short. I saw it in *The Berrigan Advocate*, and I took it out, and I kept it aside. I wrote it out, and broadcast it, and then about two weeks later, guess what appeared in *The Berrigan Advocate*? The same story – they'd lifted the story from me that I'd lifted from them! That was what country newspapers were like. There were never any reporters and there was no fear of plagiarism in those days. It was just a matter of getting what you could get from anywhere.

I did have the opportunity once, however, to report on a very big story in the area. There was a large fire at a timber mill at Mathoura, which is halfway between Echuca and Deniliquin. I had a little

2QN, George Street, Deniliquin, June 1959

At the console at 2QN Deniliquin, June 1959

portable tape recorder, one of the first of its kind, that the station had bought. So I went down there and recorded an interview with the timber mill owner, who said all was all doom, gloom and so forth. Then I drove back as fast as I could to make the news service I had at 6.30 pm on 2QN. About halfway there the Vanguard Estate car Dad had given me in lieu of pay for work on the farm broke down.

I was trying to do 70 miles an hour which was at the limits of the car – over its limits, as it turned out. Luckily, a friend of mine (he would probably be called a hoon these days) had a big powerful American car, and he towed me back to Deniliquin. I got there even faster than if I had driven myself and I just had time to

The Vanguard when it was first bought, circa *1946*

get the tape organised. We didn't have any tape recorders then so I couldn't dub it from this little tape recorder to another recorder as we did later. I lined up the little 'grab' that I wanted and started reading the introduction, reporting that I had spoken to the manager of the sawmill who said there'd been a dreadful loss. Then I held up the tape recorder to the microphone, and you heard it click on as his voice came in, and then click again as I turned it off and returned to reading. This was in 1959 or 1960, about twenty years before the ABC put in sound inserts! It was great fun and the station thought it was great too. I didn't have the opportunity or time to do this again, unfortunately. I was too busy copywriting advertisements.

In those days, only the big companies would have their own recordings to send in or scripts to be read. Remember that there were no audio tapes then and the records were either the new long-playing ones, 45s, or the 33s which were just coming in. Basically, in our little country stations, if local advertisers had anything to sell, they had to give you the details. Sometimes they would write the material

At the copywriting desk, 2QN Deniliquin, June 1959

themselves, and you'd have to rewrite it, or other times they would just come in and have a chat to you. Our salesman would also go around visiting people to sell them advertising space, and often he'd come back and say, 'Here's a whole lot of notes for Gillespie's, and this is what they want to promote.' You would then write something like, 'Now is your chance to get some of the best overseas items that are available at Gillespie's', or some such.

You had to be creative and keep the scripts varied. You also had to calculate the length so the advertisements would take exactly 15 seconds, 30 seconds or a minute to read. A minute was the longest one. So copywriting was a big part of the job. I spent most of my time basically sitting in an office at 2QN just writing stories for the news or for the advertisers. Fortunately, I was good at it.

While I was there, I also joined the Deniliquin Dramatic Club and played a half-caste Aborigine in a local production called *Fountains Beyond*. It was a great disaster. It was a story about the issues facing Aboriginal people living on the outskirts of the small town. We played that in a small town with Aboriginal people living on the outskirts. It was a bit too close to the bone and the locals got a bit uncomfortable.

By the time I had been at Deniliquin for eighteen months, I had done everything. There was no chance of promotion in such a small radio station, and I wanted to do more in the news service. I also needed a change and wanted to do something else. At 2QN I was a first-time employee, now I was a person with experience – not a terrific amount of experience, but a 'senior' broadcaster. I was ready for a step up.

I wrote to every station on the east coast of Australia, offering to help them extend their news service, and hoping I could live near the sea. I got Charleville which was 1500 km inland. I've still got a copy of every letter I sent to all those stations.

4VL CHARLEVILLE

I went to Charleville in September 1960 and stayed till March 1961. It was only six months over the summer but I worked really hard, learnt a lot and it was fun. I enjoyed the whole experience.

One of the reasons I went there was because 4VL wanted to introduce a local news service. I was not employed as a journalist, I was employed as a copywriter. As far as the news went, I was a one-man band. I compiled, wrote and read the news, and that was just one of the jobs I had. At Charleville, I did have time to go out and get the news, although again I was writing copy, being on air and going around servicing local advertisers. Sometimes we even took to the streets, using my car, to promote our sponsor's products. I remember doing this with Persil, for example. I think I did about 60 hours a week and was paid for about 40.

4VL Charleville was the only radio station in southwest Queensland. We had a huge area to cover, nearly the size of Victoria.

4VL, Wills Street, Charleville, September 1960

4VL Persil promotion, October 1964, Cliff at far right with colleagues Frank Aitcheson and Kevin Anderson in front of the Triumph Herald

There was just nothing there – such a tiny population spread over such a large area! People depended on us for their news and their entertainment as there was no TV. For many, the only voices they might hear were on the radio; the newspapers weren't as important. On radio you could hear voices all the time and they were chatting to you in your own home. We broadcast from 6.00 am in the morning and would close at 11.00 pm because everyone had gone to bed by 8.00 pm anyhow. There were a number of announcers during the day. I wasn't on-air very much at all except for the news bulletins and, to manage my long shift, I would record my 6.30 am bulletin the night before.

One of my biggest stories, as the 'radio roundsman', was about the Queensland train stoppage. We had to keep our listeners updated all day on the arrival and departure times of the trains that were running in the area. It was lucky, really, as I was flat chat at the time, that I was on the scene and able to interview the Queensland Railways Commissioner, Mr Moriarty, who was in Charleville that afternoon.

The local newspaper credited me with a 'scoop interview', and that was a buzz.

The ten-minute news service was very popular but it wasn't always easy to find enough news. I tried generally to include at least ten items, and I remember one day, I was really at my wits' end. I'd used every bit of old copy I'd put aside that I could use, and then I had a brilliant break. Down the centre of Wills Street, the main street in Charleville, was a nature strip, or a sort of median strip to divide the road. There had been some rain, so I talked about the flourishing green strip down the centre of the street. When you get to the stage of writing about grass growing on the median strip, you are getting desperate.

We were never short of horse-racing news. In those days, of course, there were no TAB agencies. The only way you could place a legal bet was at a race meeting where bookmakers operated. However, on Saturday mornings, 4VL would broadcast the horses, jockeys, and barrier numbers of all the races at meetings in Brisbane, Sydney and Melbourne. We got all the racing details from *The Courier Mail* which would arrive on the early plane at about 8.15 or 8.30 am. We would pick up a copy, go back to the studio and read it out at dictation speed, so all the illegal SP bookies throughout the whole of southwest Queensland could get the latest information, and write it all down. There just was no other form of communication in those days.

The amusing part about it was that the race details broadcasts were sponsored by some of the big sheep stations that were in the area. The script would go something like, 'Race 8, horse 10, Buggerlugs, ridden by J. Dawkins, number 5 barrier', and then, more brightly, 'This broadcast is brought to you by the So and So Sheep Station, where they have got Ramsey III standing for stud, and he is renowned for his progeny', and everything like that. You would put in these ads for the sheep stations, and then back to 'Race 9, horse 9'.

The sheep stations were particularly interested in the race reports as many SP bookies were operating on the stations. Don't forget, in those days, there were a terrific lot of station hands working on the stations before they were replaced by mechanization. Each station had a little population or village of its own, with its own SP bookie, of course. They depended totally on us for the racing guide before the races. The results were also fully reported in the daily sports broadcasts and on Saturday afternoons on a live relay from Brisbane.

I still remember my alarm one day when the plane carrying *The Courier Mail* was delayed. I went straight to the boss, and asked, 'What do I do?' He said, 'Go down and see so-and-so', who ran a shop in Charleville; a legitimate shop. I went to his house, a Queenslander on stilts, and found him underneath the house where he had a full set-up – one that would make a TAB here envious – for the locals to place their bets. He had a big two-way receiver to get the racing information. He could pick it up from Melbourne, Sydney and Brisbane radio stations. Normal receivers just couldn't do that then. He may have had telephone connections too. I don't know. He had a list of the runners, and he said to me, 'I can give you the horses, and I can give you the barrier positions. I can't give you all the jockeys, but it will keep you going, anyhow.' And it did.

We also read out the rainfall report and I remember this was one of my first jobs in Charleville. It was an important service as there weren't any bitumen roads in southwest Queensland, and too much rain can make the roads there impassable. I had a list of station names, and would have to read out, '20 points at Mallacalumbi, one inch at Tullagaroupna', or something like that. There wasn't one name I could pronounce easily in the whole list. The locals reckoned it was one of the most amusing broadcasts ever, as I struggled through this list of mainly Aboriginal or made-up names. There was no-one to call on for back-up, I just had to plough on. These names really had to be learned, and the spelling and pronunciation were sometimes two completely different things. The locals thought it was hilarious.

Signal strength was a perennial problem. Theoretically we were limited to a 2000-watt signal. However, we used to boost it to 5000 watts, working on the fact that no one would bother coming to check what we did 2000 km west of Brisbane. The best coverage we got was in the early mornings when the ionosphere conditions were right or something like that. As the day got hotter, our transmission area shrank and then at night, of course, it expanded.

We also had issues receiving signals. While I was at Charleville, I used to try to pick up the ABC which had a regional station and a regional journalist at Longreach. Because our power supply at Charleville was through a generator, I couldn't pick up outside stations when the news was on, due to the interference from the local generator. I would collect my small portable tape recorder, drive about 10 kilometres out of Charleville, turn on the news on the car radio and tape-record the ABC regional news from Longreach. From these broadcasts, I would lift whatever items were of interest to us.

4RK ROCKHAMPTON

I was very interested in reporting the news and, when an assistant journalist job became available at the ABC in Rockhampton, I applied for it. I got it because the powers that be had listened to my news services. I also had a couple of good references from the locals in Charleville, including the local newspaper proprietor – the last thing he wanted was a daily news service in his town when he only ran a weekly newspaper! I happily accepted the ABC position offered on a 'D' grading and a salary of £23.5.0 (an increase of £6 over my previous position) including a week in Brisbane before starting the job, to 'see our operations at first-hand and give you an insight into A.B.C. style and policy', as outlined in my letter of appointment in March 1961.

It was my first job as a full-time journalist. It meant going out and getting stories, working with the ABC correspondents – local people who were paid by the story – all around central Queensland, and getting to know the area well. It also meant joining the Australian Journalists' Association. They said, 'It's about time. We have been keeping an eye on you since you started at Charleville.'

There were only two of us there, Ken Newton, the regional journalist, and me. Rockhampton had a population of some 45 000 people at the time, so it was a big town and a huge rural area to cover. It was an interesting time. The main businesses were the big Vestey Meat Works, which was the main source of employment, and the shopping centre which supplied the whole of central Queensland. Everything that went out west had to come through Rockhampton. In town, we also covered the Rockhampton City Council meetings, and Livingstone Shire Council meetings. Livingstone was one of the big, rural, coastal regions around Rockhampton. Then we would call into the courts and have a look at what was going on there. There were a lot of news stories around.

In those days, sending stories was one of the most challenging undertakings imaginable by today's standards. If we wanted to send a story to the Brisbane State Newsroom, we first had to ring up the Rockhampton post office, and dictate our story, leaving out the 'a's' and the 'the's' because you had to pay per word. The telephonist there then typed it out and sent it by Morse code down to Brisbane. Rockhampton was one of the last telegraph stations to use Morse code. The story was typed out again in Brisbane. Finally, a telegram boy (no girls in those days) would hop on his bicycle and pedal out to Toowong to deliver it, or if he had any sense, he'd hop on the next train and go out that way. That's how the story got to the Newsroom in Brisbane. We could use the telephone but only in emergencies because it was very expensive. In those cases, we could dictate the story to a news typist in the office. Eventually, this process was replaced by faxes, teleprinters and now digital transmissions.

When I was working late shift, I used to finish work at eleven, and hotels were supposed to be closed at ten. However, the hotel right next to the police station was usually still open. We're talking about 1960s Queensland here where the hotel stayed open if you, shall we say, gave the appropriate observance to the appropriate legal people. In other words, slipped a few quid into their pockets. The police well and truly looked after that hotel. Occasionally I would go over there for a drink and be back at the typewriter at one o'clock with a story from the police.

There was still much lifting of stories between radio stations and newspapers. I found out about one of the funniest of these when the ABC Regional Journalist Duncan Jackson visited the Rockhampton newsroom from far western Queensland. He knew Ken Newton and, when I was introduced, he said, 'Oh, you're Cliff Peel. You used to do the news on 4VL Charleville?' I said, 'Yeah.' He said, 'Yes, I had a little trouble picking that up because of the generator at Longreach. I had to drive out about 10 kilometres in my car,' so he did exactly the same thing. So there we were, each driving out to pick up each other's news service. He said, 'I got some good items from you.'

We put on three news bulletins a day; one in the morning, one in the afternoon and one in the evening. And we didn't do too bad a job. I still remember the manager of the local newspaper getting his staff together (we weren't there, of course, but we were told about it) to give them a talking-to. He'd listened to our morning radio bulletin, got his newspaper out and found that there were four or five stories that we had that he hadn't. He wanted to know why his staff of journalists hadn't got them! We thought that fairly amusing.

ROCKHAMPTON LITTLE THEATRE

In those days, before television had reached this part of the country at least, the ABC was doing radio shows. Those were the days! ABC staff would arrange for the amateur theatre people to come and do auditions, and they would put on a radio play, which was always great fun. I auditioned and then asked the producer there whether it would be worthwhile continuing on the stage, and he said, 'Cliff, I think you're quite well paid as a journalist, aren't you?' I agreed that I was. 'And you're enjoying it?' I was enjoying it. 'Stay where you are', he said, 'you're not good enough for the stage,' which I thought was fair enough.

I enjoyed the amateur work and soon joined the Rockhampton Little Theatre. We did three or four shows there and that was a lot of fun too. We were very lucky to have a number of people in the group who had worked in English repertory before migrating to Australia. Some had even been semi-professional in England. They were quite willing to give their advice and help, so we had a very strong and successful amateur company. We could pack the big Rockhampton Town Hall, which seated 800 people, for five nights during our productions, so that wasn't too bad. I might add that it was lucky for us that there wasn't any television. We had, I won't say professional, but very high standards as an amateur group. We would rehearse for about four or five weeks before we put on a play. I remember we did *Pygmalion, Keep in a Cool Place, The Reluctant Debutante* and one where I played a Scottish diplomat. Doing the accent for that one was difficult.

Each production was reported on in the local newspaper since it was such a big part of the local entertainment. We used to take our shows on the road and performed at the Mount Morgan Theatre and the Emerald Little Theatre, some 500 kilometres away. We also entered a couple of plays in an eisteddfod. In one of these shows two of us played detectives and were dressed in suits

Cliff with the leading lady in Keep in a Cool Place, *1961*

and detective hats. Once, during rehearsal, when we had a long gap between appearances on stage, we decided to go to the pub next door and have a beer. So we did: we walked in, the two of us looking terribly like detectives, and one particular chap took one look at us, put his beer down, and disappeared straight out of the door. We must have been very convincing. I had to laugh!

SURF LIFESAVING CLUB

I liked swimming and in Rockhampton I could swim all year round. There was a beautiful, brand-new Olympic-size pool in the town. The locals found it far too cold to swim in the winter in Queensland, but for me and another southerner, a doctor at the hospital, it was warm even in May, June, July and August. At lunch time, we would have this marvellous 50-metre pool to ourselves to swim up and down, lap upon lap, completely uninterrupted by anyone else. I wasn't a fast swimmer, but I was a strong swimmer. I could just keep going at a steady pace.

I also joined the Surf Lifesaving Club in Emu Park in the late summer of 1961. While Rockhampton wasn't on the coast, the Surf Lifesaving Club, some 40 kilometres away at Emu Park, was within reach. The nearest seaside resort for Rockhampton is Yeppoon, to the north-east of the city, and Emu Park is slightly south of Yeppoon. I often spent the weekend at Emu Park. The accommodation was pretty basic, and the early morning swim was obligatory if you had used the Clubhouse. It was very convenient to stay there.

The beach was patrolled on Saturday and Sunday, with about eight people on patrol at once. If they had to go into the water to help someone, they could use the reels, go out and rescue them and pull them back in. One person would swim out, possibly with a back-up swimmer, and four people were needed on the line to drag them in. Also, as soon as the rescued person was within wading distance, someone would be needed to assist them – help them out of the water, mouth-to-mouth resuscitation, whatever was required. We never had anyone drown on our patrolled beach, fortunately.

One of the lifesavers' duties was to check for sharks before opening the beach to swimmers. What we were told in those days was that there were very few sharks close to the beach because the reef was a fair way out. Occasionally we saw one or two. Sometimes someone on the balcony would see a fin in the water and give the alert.

Emu Park beach with Surf Lifesaving Clubhouse at left, 1962

Before we opened the beach, Club members who had stayed overnight would have the obligatory 100-metre swim at six o'clock in the morning. The deal was that you could stay at the Club overnight for two shillings, but you were required to do the six o'clock swim. It was a good way of sobering up after a hard night! Then the surf boat would go out as a precaution, just to have a bit of a look around.

The surf boat had six rowers and the steerer, who was the boat captain. One day, during my second summer at the Club, the boat crew was on the water for a practice session, and they gave the shark signal – the rowers all put their oars up in the air. I was doing the broadcast through the loudspeaker at the time, playing taped music and advertisements. This was a way to make a bit of money for the Club, and many clubs did it then and still do. When I saw the shark I immediately dropped the recording and put the siren on. The beach patrol blew their whistles, told everyone to get out of the water, and closed the beach. They pulled up the flags and crossed them, which indicated that the beach was closed until we got the 'all clear'.

The local policeman came, and agreed that the beach should be closed. The routine then was for the crew to paddle around until the sharks disappeared out to sea. We allowed a quarter of an hour or so, and did a few sweeps up and down scanning with binoculars to see if the shark was still visible anywhere. It only happened once in my time at the Club.

Every weekend there would also be training for inter-club competitions and then Central Queensland District competitions. The winners would go to State competitions. One year we qualified for the Queensland State Competition. We had a winning 'march past' team at Broadbeach, and I was staying at its surf club. It was the same arrangement – to use the accommodation, you had to do a patrol. The surf on the Gold Coast is a lot more ferocious than at Emu Park, and I didn't like the look of it, so I worked out there wouldn't be too many swimmers at six o'clock in the morning. That was a good time to go out and patrol: any swimmers would be good swimmers and wouldn't need rescuing.

The beach at Emu Park is protected by the reef, and also by the offshore islands which keep the swell down. The waves are not very large as a result. I was not a great surfer, but being a surf lifesaver trained me a lot. The gentle surf of Emu Park suited me well, since I mostly wanted to meet people and make friends through the Club.

My social life in Rockhampton was mostly on the weekends. As a member of the Surf Club, I would have company for drinks on Saturday night. We would be patrolling or training on Saturdays and

Emu Park SLC 'march past' team at Tannum Sands SLC Carnival, February 1963

Sundays, and occasionally we'd have a meeting during the week. Being captain of one of the patrols meant that I had to ensure that I had enough people for the patrol, and to turn up on time! It was also my job to train the patrol members so that they knew what to do if someone got stung by a jellyfish or something of that kind.

Once, in a little bay on an unpatrolled beach near the Surf Club, a child went swimming and drowned. We looked for her but we didn't find her. We don't know where it happened, or what happened there; there may have been a rip. Not many people used the beach. It wasn't a particularly good one.

During my time in Rockhampton, I completed my bronze medallion and got my instructor's certificate. I also did a lot of PR for the Club. One of our patrol teams won the 'march past' in the District competition, but I wasn't in that team. At that time surf lifesaving was only for men. There were no female lifesavers, or juniors of either sex, in those days.

The beach at Emu Park was never packed with crowds of people like city beaches. It was really only used by locals, and most people came by car so there were hardly any children or teenagers without adults. There's a branch line from Rockhampton to Emu Park, and for many, many years the miners from Mt Morgan had their annual picnic there. Special trains brought literally hundreds of miners to that picnic. Those days were gone before I arrived in Rockhampton, but I did see the big railway shunting yards there. The train only ran once a day in each direction. I took it one day just to have the fun of it but it left pretty early in the afternoon – earlier than the beach patrol finishing time. So I used to drive.

Little red sports car

When I came to Rockhampton from Charleville, I had a Triumph Herald sedan. These cars were imported from England. They were very reliable and well-made cars. Later, they were made in Australia by Australian Motor Industries. When the news broke in 1961 that this company had got into financial trouble, I had a phone call from the local dealer, asking me to sell him my Herald and buy a Triumph convertible from him in exchange.

So I got this brand new red sports car. However, I soon found out why the dealer was keen to shift it. The quality control on the Australian-made cars was terrible. Once, one of the front wheels came off, for no reason at all. And the doors always gave trouble, the exhaust came apart – it was not a well-constructed car at all. But I did get a lot of attention in that car. As one of my friends commented, it was an excellent 'pick-up truck'!

I had great fun with it. I am horrified by this now, but I found that I could drive standing up, hanging on to the windscreen with one hand and on to the steering wheel with the other, standing on one foot and using the other for the accelerator or brake as needed. I got a much better view of the road especially if there was lot of traffic

Triumph Herald convertible at Emu Park SLC, August 1961

ahead. It was one of my little party tricks. Luckily I never crashed doing this.

Sunday nights were often a bit hectic, because I had to be singing in the church choir at 7.30 pm. The bar at the Emu Park Hotel opened unofficially (illegally, if you insist) at 4.00 pm for thirsty lifesavers and anyone else. The deal was that the pub could open for a couple of hours as long as we behaved ourselves. There was only one policeman at the police station in Emu Park, and at about 6.00 or 6.30 pm there was usually a phone call from the policeman's wife to the pub owner Dick Tennant, who was also the local ABC correspondent. The conversation went like this: 'Is my husband there?' 'I don't know.' 'Oh. He'll be there shortly. Can you tell him that I just called?' And that was the hint to close the pub, and for me to join the choir for the evening service. I don't know what the lady in the row in front of me thought about my beery breath every Sunday evening!

The choir was a good way to meet people, and so was the local theatre group. My work took me out and about, of course. Once,

I went to cover a rugby match. I said to the regional journalist, 'I haven't got the faintest idea what this game is about, I've only seen one in my life.' He told me not to worry, and that I'd soon pick it up. I was helped by the journalist from the local paper. On another occasion, I was covering a meeting of the Synod of the Anglican Church of Central Queensland. The Archbishop of Brisbane was in attendance. The Synod was held at a hall about a kilometre away from the main centre of town. When the day's meeting was finished at about 4.00 pm, they were wondering how to get back into town. The Dean of Rockhampton, whom I knew quite well, asked me, 'Cliff, can you give the Archbishop and me a lift back?' And I replied, 'Well, I've got a convertible!' That was all right with them, so I had the Archbishop of Brisbane and the Dean of Rockhampton in full regalia in the back seat of my 'pick-up truck' as I drove back – with the top down, I might add.

I did have an accident with the Triumph convertible. I was driving to Melbourne on holiday with my sister and her friend on board. We planned to stay the night in Surfer's Paradise, and were driving along the Pacific Highway. I was wearing a pair of thongs, which I normally didn't wear while driving. Arriving at the narrow bridge that used to cross the Nerang River, the car in front stopped suddenly. I tried to stop, but my thong got caught between the brake pedal and the accelerator pedal. So there was a bit of a crunch, and my car had to be towed away. It took the tow truck 30 minutes to get to us because of the blocked road. No need to guess what caused the blockage.

I managed to do some running repairs to the car, straightened a few bits out, and put a leather strap around the bonnet to hold it all together so I could drive the girls back to Melbourne. The other car was not damaged. So much for the Australian-built Triumph. When I returned to Rockhampton, I traded it in – what was left of it – and bought myself a second-hand Holden.

I liked Rocky and I would have stayed on except that the regional journalist was a younger chap than me, he had a family and he looked like he wasn't going to move. Quite often this happens in regional newsrooms: people like the area, they know the area, it's their patch and they're quite happy to stay there. And Ken Newton looked like he was going to stay put. There was no chance of promotion or advancement so I watched the ABC bulletins each month to check out the new positions. When it came up, I applied for a position at the ABC in Sale in Victoria.

3GI SALE

I accepted the position of 'C' Grade Journalist at Sale in December 1962. This was a newly created position, because ABC was expanding their newsroom there and was a promotion for me with a salary of £29.2.0. I was the Assistant Journalist to the Regional Journalist Neil Munro. In those days there were only two of us to cover the whole of Gippsland. Neil was only a year older than me, and soon became a very good friend of mine. He is still a very good friend. He was a really large chap, a former newspaper journalist and originally from New Zealand, and we got on very well. I had a good time down there.

The role at Sale was very similar to the one I had at Rockhampton. We had morning, midday and early evening bulletins to produce, the same as in Rockhampton. We worked a day and an evening shift, with an overlap in the middle. There was always someone there from eight in the morning until eleven at night to cover and back up the three news bulletins per day. These were read by the newsreader who was usually also the station manager.

One of the best examples of newsreading I have seen was by visiting relief manager John Sloane, who is now deceased. There are a lot of stories about him. He was a senior announcer in Melbourne, so he had to read the news and undertake the managerial duties, whatever they were. On one occasion, he read the midday news, then he went out for, shall we say, a 'short' lunch with some friends of his from the East Sale air base. At eight minutes to seven that evening, I was waiting for John to come in and read the news. I had the feeling that I might have to read the news myself, which did happen in emergencies occasionally when someone was ill. When John came in – wafted in – from lunch, he picked up the news, sat down, opened the mike and read seven minutes of it without a stumble, without a slur, without anything out of place, and he'd never seen it before! He was renowned for that, his ability to just turn it on. He was the ultimate newsreader. That's not bad for an afternoon, shall we say, of socializing.

In those days, before tape recorders, sound inserts or film for television, we didn't go out much to get the stories. Unless, of course, there was something really major and I can't recall anything like that while I was there. We didn't have any transport either; we didn't have a station car, and if we did use our own car it generally had to be authorized by Melbourne first. We could get a mileage payment but we mainly stayed in the offices. We might walk around to the Mayor's office, or other offices in Sale for local news.

We mainly received stories by phone or else by telex. We had a whole range of correspondents in every major town and even some of the villages. They were local people who became ABC local correspondents. They were good at going around and having a gossip and finding out what was happening; some were very good and kept sending us in stories that I rather enjoyed and we got good news coverage. Our best informants were people in key positions, like the local policeman's wife. They'd send us in the stories and were paid for them. I think they were paid five shillings or something like that. In those days it wasn't bad money. We really relied a lot on them. The items ranged from court cases to fines, accidents and also important local stories about rural news and local council matters.

Before computers and the digital age, we spent most of our time getting the stories and writing them up on a typewriter. Before I got there, when Neil was on his own, there was only the evening news service. When I arrived they put in the morning and midday news services. We had been trying to get a new typewriter – we did have two but one of them had some keys missing, and was very old. Anyway, one day there was a terrible accident. When Neil was cleaning the newsroom, he put the typewriter on the windowsill, and made sure that the window was open. Somehow, the typewriter lost its balance and crashed to the street below. We got a new typewriter. We checked that there was no-one in the street at the time, I might add.

Typing was very important in radio and in the newsroom. I spent half my time in front of a typewriter typing and, fortunately, I was good. I had taught myself when I was still at the Vincent School of Broadcasting. I bought a little typewriter and just typed. I tried to read the manual, but couldn't make sense of it so I just taught myself. I only used about two or three fingers on each hand. I could keep up with a professional typist later when I was working in the television newsroom and occasionally when things got a bit hectic, I helped to type out items and things like that. I was pretty fast because I could keep up with the correspondents reading in their reports rather than taking the stories down as hand-written notes.

I had a very good relationship with Neil. We worked as a team and shared a lot of jokes, sometimes practical jokes. I also got on well with his little dog that came into the studio. Not many people did. When things got really busy in the office and there were lots of stories coming in from everywhere we would prioritise what we were doing and divide up the stories. Neil, being the regional journalist, would look after the Melbourne stories. We were such a good team. I found out later that Neil thought we were so successful that he continued the same pattern – the same working relationship – with all the journalists he worked with subsequently in the Sale office over the next thirty years!

Perhaps most importantly, Neil introduced me to the glories of wine. He had an old 1939 Hudson, a big 'Yank tank', and every now and again we'd go to the Sale railway station and collect five- or ten-gallons casks, big wooden barrels, that had been sent down from

Neil Munro and Cliff in the 3GI–ABV4 Newsroom, September 1963

De Bortoli Wines in Griffith, New South Wales. This intrigued the railway staff. They'd come to watch Neil put these barrels into the boot of the Hudson, which we would take back to bottle at his place. Now in the 1960s in Sale there weren't that many wine drinkers so we used beer bottles. There were plenty of them, that's the big beer bottles, which were 26 fluid ounces (750 ml). We would sterilize them by heating them in the oven. Then, after they'd cooled down, we'd put the wine in. We couldn't get corks or screw tops, then so we used crown seals. To make sure this would work, we rang up the original Dan Murphy, the real man who was running his own shop in Chapel Street, Windsor in those days. 'If only everyone would do the same thing,' he said. 'Crown seals are just ideal for wine. Why they aren't used I don't know.' That was in about 1962. I remember too that there would be a few raised eyebrows when the wine in beer bottles was served at dinner parties that Neil and his wife Joan would host. Joan was a really good cook and I was always glad to be invited along.

After hours, I had plenty of spare time to explore the area, especially at weekends. Any news stories in Gippsland were covered from Melbourne. If Neil was going away for the weekend, he would just ask me to keep an eye out and if anything happened to let Melbourne know. I often travelled alone or with a friend or a casual acquaintance I'd met in Sale. I'd team up with itinerant people, bankers, schoolteachers and similar short-term residents who also had the weekend off, but mainly I travelled by myself.

Neil had a block of land on Dargo Road at Briagolong – Valencia Creek, actually, to be precise. Neil's car had a trailer and we'd take a little pedal organ, numerous friends and numerous bottles of red wine and have a little barbecue and sing hymns and other ditties. Now, the Dargo Road was a treacherous narrow little gravel road. The saying was that if you didn't leave Dargo with some sort of alcoholic reinforcement, the road was pretty scary. We would see the occasional traveller – after dealing with about 30 or 40 kilometres of hairpin bends, the gravel road and an occasional log truck – come around the bend to suddenly hear a group of people singing hymns. We never knew of anyone running off the road, but they may have wondered where they had ended up! It was very isolated. That stays in my mind, those hymn-singing sessions on the Dargo Road in Valencia Creek on this block of scrub land and a little bit of a clearing, no house or anything. And, of course, once you took off the crown seal, you couldn't put it back so you had to drink the whole bottle.

Most of the time I used to go by train to Melbourne to spend the weekend, catching up with friends, mucking around, getting into trouble. Well, not much trouble. I never got myself arrested. It took about four or five hours by train which was easier than by car. I stayed with my sister. She had a flat in Kew at the time. Other times I'd stay with just acquaintants. Occasionally I'd hire a room for the night. I didn't usually have firm plans. On Monday morning I'd come back on the Gippsland train and get down to Sale in good time for the 2.00 pm shift. The beauty about it was you could have bacon and eggs on the train on the buffet along with beer. So I'd always have my early morning beers at 10.00 am and arrive at Sale about midday in a fairly good mood for work.

I joined the Sale Repertory Group and did a few little trips around the area with them. I performed in three plays while I was there. The group was active and had a membership of 45 and growing. I played Felix Dulay, the husband of the leading actress in *My Three Angels*, and both produced a one-act play and played the character Tony Sugden in *The Badger Game* in July 1963 as part of a state-wide festival held in Traralgon.

The plays were often reviewed, quite critically, in the local paper which was fun. I had a minor role in *Bonadventure* and did earn a mention in the group of actors 'who were good to a lesser extent', as reviewed in *The Gippsland Times* – which was not so bad compared to less favourable comments:

TEA WILL BE SERVED IN THE SUPPER ROOM

SALE REPERTORY GROUP

presents

"The Badger Game"

(By Kenneth Horne)

Cast in Order of Appearance:

Tony Sugden - - - - - CLIFF PEEL
Joe Banks - - - - GEORGE WARNER
Yvonne Banks (his wife) - PAT WEISSMANN

Producer: CLIFF PEEL

Stage Manager: NAN McINTOSH

The Badger Game program, 1963

It was a pity ... it was only a one-night performance. Perhaps Sale Repertory Group's cast would have settled down, removing the marked tendency, especially in the opening, to overact. This caused humour where pathos and tension was intended. Consequently, there was a lowering in the dramatic pitch and this was not easily restored.

Our group was also struggling behind the scenes and in front of

Sale Repertory Group, Cliff seated in centre of front row, December 1963

house with the lack of repairs and lack of cleaning at our main venue, the Sale Memorial Hall. Being a journalist, I was also persuaded to lead a community campaign about this alarming and neglectful state of affairs. I wrote several letters which were published in the Letters to the Editor section of the newspaper, suggesting a round-table conference between the relevant parties to address the issue and several methods of fundraising that Council could pursue. We got Council a bit fired up about it, but nothing happened while I was still in Sale.

I was also involved in the Sale Junior Chamber of Commerce and became President. We supported the work of some local charities, organised guest speakers, and held debates. I remained a member of the Young Farmers' Association so I was never short of social activities.

Regional television came to Gippsland in 1964 with the opening of ABV4, the Gippsland television station of the ABC. Actually this was just a relay station with no studios and the signals came from microwave towers. Locally, we just had to provide an engineer to make sure the technical equipment worked properly on the towers as everything came from Melbourne.

Although we didn't have a direct role in the television relay, we did talk to our colleagues in Melbourne. One day, the television news supervisor visited Sale and asked me if I would be interested in moving to Melbourne to work in the television newsroom which was being expanded. I hesitated for one second and said, 'Yes!' My formal application was accepted in August 1964. This was a timely opportunity for me as, knowing that my future at Sale was limited, I had started to look around. I was happy in Sale but Neil wasn't going anywhere, and never did, and I would have been an Assistant there forever. So I was quite happy to broaden my career and go into television news, which by that time was really starting to develop.

From left, Regional Journalist Neil Munro, Rural Officer at Sale Philip Lamb and his wife Julie, Victorian News Editor Jack Taylor and Cliff, at the opening of ABV4, Sale, 1964

Chapter Six

ABV2 TV MELBOURNE

Before I could leave Sale, I had to get someone to replace me. This could have been a problem but fortunately Neil found someone who was willing to move from the local paper to radio in much the same way that he had done. So within three weeks of accepting the new

ABV2 Ripponlea studios in Gordon Street, Melbourne, circa *1965*

job, I arrived in Melbourne and quickly found a place to live close by. I rented a unit in Blenheim Street, East St Kilda, between Windsor and Balaclava stations, not far from the ABC's Ripplonlea studios in Gordon Street, Elsternwick. I could walk or take the train, and later found riding a bike was my best option.

I was transferred to Melbourne on the same classification, C grade journalist, with a salary of £30.17.0 and a loading of 30 shillings per week in lieu of penalty rates for working at weekends. In addition, I received six weeks' holiday per year which was a huge bonus. Most importantly, it allowed me to expand my travel plans, which I did, travelling around North Queensland for five weeks in September that year. The trip took in Cairns, Port Douglas, Magnetic Island, Townsville and many other places, and I also fitted in a visit to Rockhampton to see old friends.

LEARNING ABOUT TELEVISION

Television in Australia was introduced in November 1956 just in time for the Olympic Games. There was pressure on the government to allow television, because it was already a big thing in the United States and Britain. You've got to remember that in those days the government was a lot more conservative and they were very worried about this newfangled television thing and its effects on morality. If you look back in the newspapers of those days, you will see lots of stories about the ill effects of television. Pornography and all sorts of things could happen through this dreadful thing called television! The government had to regulate it first before they allowed it on the unsuspecting public. It had to be well and truly under control.

Coming back to news services, I don't think the commercial television stations had very many news services. They started off basically reading from newspapers; it was just like radio with faces. There were rules limiting the number of advertisements and time per hour spent on them. I think there were even stricter rules when television first came in. Also, there weren't many people trained in television work – people who knew what to do. This is what I found in news, even in the mid-1960s when I went into television. Don't forget it had been only ten years since the first broadcasts were made and people were still finding their way.

SCRIPT WRITING FOR TELEVISION

My first job at ABV2 was to learn how to script news films. You would be given a 30-second or 45-second film and the details provided by the news reporter. You would then write a short introduction and then the story script that the newsreader would read over the film. This was the most simple method, and the preferred one. Very rarely did we record a voice-over. There were two ways of having sound then. One was using a sound camera in which the sound was recorded on the film. The journalist, using a microphone, would interview the subject and the interview would be filmed and recorded. This was the easiest method and, although the quality was poorer, it was good enough for TV news. Alternatively, you used the system where the film was used with audio tape in sync: you sent out a cameraman and a sound recordist along with the journalist so you'd have a crew of three. One would be holding a camera, one holding a tape recorder, and the journalist would say, 'Take one!' and click the clapperboard – that click allows you to get the sound and the picture in sync. It was a bit fiddly and time-consuming. Basically, if you could avoid it, you did, which meant I did a lot of script writing.

Fortunately, I was very good at scripting. I was fast and I enjoyed it. Often, we had the overseas films coming in at 4.00 pm, flying in from London, Europe, or the US. We didn't have too much time to choose the ones we wanted. We had a list of the films and a basic summary of what was on them. We knew which films we could prioritise and leave for the 7.00 pm news because we didn't have time to sit around and look at all those happy snappies. We had to pick out the ones that were most important and most relevant to the day's news. There were no voice-overs or very, very few, so we virtually had to script them all. I think, at most, I did ten or maybe even twelve short films once between 4.00 pm and 6.00 pm. We did one draft and that was it. We had to be speedy and good typists, and you didn't have time to think too much. They didn't call me 'Cliché Cliff' for nothing!

First of all, I'd watch the film, then shot-list it. That means to calculate the length of the shot (for example three seconds long equalled three feet long) and then to calculate the number of words needed per foot. In writing the script for a film, each sentence was supposed to correspond with the image on the screen. As a certain image came up, the producer would press the cue button, which would flash on the newsreader's desk, who would start reading that sentence so it would synchronise with the film being shown.

The newsreader would have about twenty pages of stories to read for a half-hour news service. I remember one of the announcers had a habit of folding everything in a nice little neat pile and then would put it in front of him. The only trouble was just before he sat down, as the news theme was playing, he went to put his papers down but missed the desk and the papers went on the floor. The camera opened up with an empty desk. Suddenly a head comes up saying, 'I'll be with you in a moment,' in a beautiful cultured ABC voice. It was one of the most delightful things I've seen.

The pages were numbered, of course, from one to twenty with one item per page. The reason for that is if the film suddenly breaks down, or if you run out of time, you can get the floor manager in the studio to tell the newsreader to go to number six or drop five, for example. If it was the end of the bulletin, we would be looking at the time and the timing. We didn't have time before the bulletin to time the things. Every story had a length of time on it, of course. They can vary by seconds. Suddenly when you're coming to the end of the bulletin and, in case something happens, you need a range of little, spare items to choose from – padding, we called it.

We aimed to end up with one final item which had a bit of strength to it so you could go out with a bang before you throw to the weatherman, the same as they do these days too. What you do is you look at your clock, and think, no, we haven't got time for those three items. You have two ways of letting the decision be known, through the floor manager in the studio or else you have a cut button. When you press the button, it cuts all the sound off except your voice booming across the studio, 'Go to twelve.' The graphics are also numbered for the item that they're concerned with. The announcer might look up but the viewers would never notice. We had to adjust our timing in practically every news bulletin, even if it was just one item. It became second nature. You gave yourself a pat on the back if you ever went straight through without any problems.

Producing the news

In the news studio, the floor manager made sure everything on the set worked smoothly and that the news reader was looking at the right camera. News wasn't terribly complicated. If you were a floor manager of a big production, that was completely different. You would be flat chat. The main action was controlled by the director or producer of the news bulletin. I often acted in this role and it was pretty nerve-racking because you're doing a half-hour unrehearsed, live show. If anything happens, you've got to sort it out.

I've always been confused about whether I *produced* a news program or *directed* a news program. I think I was producing them – the term meant different things to different people. You have your news bulletins in the order they're supposed to be read. Then you get in the studio, sit there and get the items going, making sure the right film comes down at the right time from the right chain. You had a mixer sitting next to you. He was the one who would put the picture on the screen to be sent out, transmitted. You'd say, 'Okay, take camera one.' Then you'd give an order to upstairs, 'Roll film.' Then you'd say, 'Take line one,' or 'line two' or whichever's coming in. When it's the end of the film, you had to look for your little cue dots to show that the film has gone in, and then you'd say, 'Okay, take camera one,' or 'Take one.' You used shortcuts because you all spoke the same language.

These days, all the graphics and everything are digitised. I don't know how they do it. In those days, if you wanted to put a graph or a slide on air (we used slides as well) again you'd have to have your slides lined up. We also could superimpose the name of the person talking or being shown at the bottom of the screen. That would be done from the studio. They would have a little bit of cardboard with the name written on it, say Bob Hawke or Sir Robert Menzies, or Prime Minister Menzies, or something like that. The camera would take a photo of that and you'd superimpose that on the film. That's when the mixer would superimpose camera two over film. This is what I was learning. It was great and it was fun. It was a new world because radio's only sound. This is vision and sound.

Also in those days, we were experimenting, trying out new techniques. We even got some journalists to stand up in front of the camera and talk, which was something very new in those days. (Nowadays, of course, you can't keep them off the cameras.) There weren't very many journalists who were good at it – they'd never been trained. The journalists would go out with the cameraman and the sound recordist, get the film, come back, and write up a story for us. Then we'd listen to the tape. If they interviewed people, we would then also have some pictures to illustrate the story as well – say they're opening a new factory or something like that. We'd have shots of the factory. We'd have film of the minister saying the appropriate words, or explaining what they were going to do there and so on. You'd have his voice and a headshot. I'd script the intro and whatever the announcer had to read up to the time that we cut to the person. Or, while he was explaining something, you'd run another film over the top. We did a lot of mixing and could cover a lot of stuff. When videotape came in, it was much easier because you didn't have to send the film to the lab for processing. That saved so much time. Basically, if you had a good cameraman, you could practically take the videotape out of his machine and put it on air – no editing required. For something like a house fire, they would have a broad shot and a close-up, another shot, maybe only 30 or 40 seconds in total. That's all you needed for a news bulletin.

I enjoyed both scripting and producing the news and occasionally I went out reporting too, but I was not a good reporter. I felt more at home handling the material that came in and I was probably better at writing than I was at doing on-camera work or working in the field. My stronger points were sub-editing, scriptwriting, and also being Chief of Staff and organising the whole coverage – which I started doing at ABC TV. Those four years were very, very rewarding. My work at that time really let me use all the skills I had developed in the radio days, and on stage, and I learned a lot of new things.

My chief of staff role

When I had to act as Chief of Staff, I had to come in early, read the newspapers and read all the latest bulletins coming in on the teleprinter from overseas. Next I would check the diary which detailed what's happening: for instance, the Prime Minister's calling a press conference at 10.00 am. I'd send my political reporter and the crew to cover that. You knew some of the things that were going on. You'd say, 'Well, look, let's go pretty light on that. Better get some film from somewhere or other.' You'd see that there was a fashion show on or something similar where you could get some film to fill the gaps.

I would also liaise with the new supervisor on the day's news priorities. On one famous occasion, we both got it wrong – initially at least. I mentioned that I was going to send a crew along to cover the Beatles when they came out on the balcony at the Southern Cross

The Beatles at the Southern Cross Hotel, Melbourne, June 1964

Hotel during their Australian tour in 1964. My television news supervisor, who was a bit staid and wasn't quite up with the Beatles, said, 'It's just a pop group, don't worry about covering that!' And of course, the next thing, it had become such a big event that I just had to get my crew in as fast as possible. I sent them off with the words, 'Just shoot and see what you can get'. The news supervisor agreed too. The crew did a good job. We didn't get the best positions so some other commercial stations were a bit ahead of me on that one. In those days you made your own decisions; there were no formal meetings or anything like that, just conversation about whether we would or wouldn't cover something. The supervisor's office was right by mine, so if I had made a decision that I thought better of, I could also change my decision quickly – which was nothing unusual.

You'd also check with your regional journalists around Victoria about any major happening. They generally notified you in the first place that they had a major event on, opening a new dam or something. We'd have a stringer there – a freelance cameraman who we would pay only by the job. These freelance camera men lived locally and had other jobs, but generally they were good news cameramen and women.

I remember we had a particular lady stringer up at Albury. She was very good. There was a terrible bus accident there. She was so great; she took the shots of the wrecked interior of the bus and pretty gruesome stuff it was too. The journalists in the regional office sent us down the story. We'd get the film and write the story using the journalist's material and script the film from that. The Chief of Staff would arrange for that as well, so you'd have some stories around the place that would come in and give enough stuff to fill a bulletin.

We had about four staff on the subs desk dealing with stories that would have two or three top reporters and one and two others. Then there was the Chief of Staff, who was me occasionally. Sometimes I would be put on a sub-editing shift for the late news, in which case I worked until about 11.00 pm or midnight. I would go in at 2.00 or 3.00 pm, depending on when the late news was on. When I was Chief of Staff, I came in early to work out what stories I was going to cover, and which journalists would go and do it. So I'd be in at 6.00 am, and go through all the material until 2.00 pm. Eventually I changed to a four-day week instead of five days and worked 10 hours a day so I could be there when most of the film had arrived for the 7.00 pm news. We had another chap who did three 11-hour shifts over the weekend; there were fewer people to help with sub-editing, and so he wouldn't start so early. He would probably have worked from 7.00 am to 6.00 pm. It wasn't always very busy on the weekend; when I had the long shift, I used the spare time to learn a foreign language.

There's a horse in the studio!

I vividly remember producing the news one night on a weekend in the late 1960s, when Jocelyn Terry was the announcer. She was a very good and experienced presenter. Normally on weekdays we had our own particular dedicated news studio, but on weekends they generally had a crew there filming an ABC production and that crew would use the big studios. To save money sometimes, they just moved an abbreviated news set into the corner of this major studio and we used the studio camera crew for the news. On this particular night, I had a rather agitated floor manager coming up to me about 6.45 pm, saying, 'Cliff, we've got a problem!' I replied with, 'Oh yeah, so what's new', or some flippant remark. He said, 'There's a horse in the studio!' I said, 'Well, take it out!' 'We can't,' he said, 'we gave it some tranquilliser, we've tranquillised it a bit too much, and it's asleep!' Anyhow, I told Jocelyn to 'find out as much you can about the horse and the production, and if it wakes up during a news bulletin, I'll get you to explain (to ad lib) what's happening. Also, if it's not being too indecent, I'll put a camera on the horse as it is being led away.' Thank goodness it was on the weekend, so we had only to provide a fifteen-minute bulletin, and happily the horse slept through the whole process.

Getting the film back

One of the greatest challenges at the time when I was working as Chief of Staff was getting the film back in time because, unlike today, we didn't have any microwave signals to plug in. Film had to physically return to the studio or to the laboratory, either from the cameramen or the stringers. We had to get the film to the studio at Ripponlea (from wherever it was filmed, all around Victoria) and we had to get it back quickly. We used to use the trains quite a lot but not the railway parcel post. Rather, we took the film to the guard, and gave him a bit of folding money. One of our drivers would go to meet the train at the other end to get the film and the guard would get another, shall we say, 'thank-you note'. So it was a private arrangement. We tried to send film by the railway parcel system, but the film could end up in Western Australia six weeks later. We had to 'privatise' this bit of the transport link – it was often the only way we could do it.

We also used aeroplanes if there were local flights, for instance from Mildura to Melbourne. But there again they were very limited, often only one flight a day. If you missed that you could put it on the overnight train and have it a day later. If it was a day late it didn't matter, because it would be the first time people would see the film anyhow. The *Herald-Sun* had several planes that used to go around Victoria delivering the early editions of the afternoon paper. We could use that service; when the plane came back to Moorabbin we'd collect the film from the pilot.

The pilots would be gently asked if they'd like to take a thank-you note with the film, so there were no problems. At that time, Channel 7 was owned by the *Herald-Sun* (HSV Seven, the Herald-Sun Victoria). The funniest part was, years later I was talking to a chap who was Chief of Staff at the same time that I was. He asked, 'How did you get your film back from the country so easily and so quickly?' I told him, 'It was quite simple, I used the *Herald-Sun* plane.' He exclaimed, 'You used the *what*!' He said he'd never have thought of that.

There was another little gimmick we used particularly for getting film from Gippsland. It was hard in those days, because the trains were a lot slower and less frequent than they are now. Our stringer there would go to a local garage that sold petrol. A car would pull up to get petrol, and the stringer would ask, 'Are you going to Melbourne?' If they were, the stringer would ask them to take the film to a particular address, and the driver would get a little reward for doing that. We used any method that we could.

I remember too the anti-Vietnam War demonstrations in 1970, 1971. These demos disrupted the city hugely. They were usually still going at 5.00 pm, when we had to get the film to Ripponlea. Traffic was blocked, no-one could move, you couldn't get past the Swanston Street city square, as it was then. One time, I remember,

I said to a journalist covering the marches, 'Okay, look, just get on a Sandringham train at Flinders Street station, and bring the film with you that way.' So that time we used the suburban train service. I told the bosses in Sydney about this once, and they were horrified. 'Oh, we would have sent a car!' I said, 'Yeah, okay, fair enough. You do that but we can't!' If we were sending film to Sydney, we had to send it by coaxial cable. That meant processing the film first, and then sending it. In the days before microwave links the cable was the only way. The studio in Sydney recorded it and replayed it, so they were always a bit iffy about making sure the film was on time.

Preparing the film

Once the film was back, it still had to be processed at the lab, which generally took about half an hour, and returned to the studio, often still wet. We would then put it on reels and edit it by splicing, cutting and rejoining the film as needed. We used three reels of film to produce the news bulletin. Once you spliced a film on, you got film A, then film B and film C all on one line. You can't alter your order unless you spool right through one film and that takes time. You haven't got time! You'd have film one, two, and three on that reel, and that's the one you put into the studio. Then you have film four, five, and six on another reel, and that's the second input into the studio. You can then go from film one, say, to film four because that's on a different reel. Then you could go back to film two on that reel. You can't change the order; you've got to follow on to whatever's the next film because they're all physically spliced together. You can skip from one reel to the next, and fast forward on a reel but it was not very fast.

In the 1960s, we didn't have videotape. It was so much easier when videotape came in – we didn't have to process it or splice it. But in those days we only had film, and film would come in during the day. We had a little diagram which told us which film was on which reel and the order they were in. Basically you could rewind or fast forward only within the short periods of time you had. I remember once someone mixed up the films and the reels they should have been on. So I said, 'I will see the first frame of each film and I can guess which is which, hopefully.' I had a pretty good idea, since I had already seen the film when I scripted it. I was good at multi-tasking and managing the reels, an area I was to specialise in later in my career.

Because it took time to actually put the film on the reel and splice it all together, you had a bit of time to type out the list of what was on each reel. Some films would come in in the morning, so we'd be able to get them out of the way on one reel. When the late stuff came in, you'd put that on as a separate reel, and then reel three might be the one film which comes in very, very late.

The cut-off time depended on the strength of the film – in other words, the strength of the story. If the film was very late but it was a very strong story, we would put that on the late news so that we had time to muck around with it. But if it was a breaking story and the film had come straight from the lab, occasionally we wouldn't even edit it; we would rely on the cameramen to edit it in the camera. You would then take a 10-second shot, stop the camera, go on to another angle, get another 10 or 15 seconds, and so on. One of the things you had to risk was what they call a 'camera flash'. There might be one little frame that has no picture on it at all and it just comes up as a flash. The film would come straight from the Cinevex laboratories, who were exceptionally good, in Gordon Street, Elsternwick, very near ABV2. Occasionally they didn't have time to even put the film through a drier and it would have the odd blotch of water, but because the film was right up to date and it was a very important story, you lived with it. Today, of course, you get instant electronic images from around the world.

In those days, our overseas film came in generally on the Qantas flight from London, which arrived in Melbourne about 3.30–4.00 in the afternoon. The time lag was about 24 hours. It depended on where the film came from; less time if we picked it up coming in from Singapore but with the European news you could be more than a day out. We still ran it, because it was the first film we had. In the very old days, when photos came out by ship, they would still be printed in magazines or newspapers even if they were three months old, because it would be the first time people had seen them. Before television, you went to see newsreels at the cinema, and there the stories could be anything up to a week old.

The point is these are the first pictures, so they do matter. What we did is when we got the latest wire stories to go with our 24-or 30-hour-old film, we updated the stories with the film. I will say that I was good at scriptwriting; I did love a good cliché.

Editing the news stories

There were a few story types that we would have to edit carefully. We were not allowed to show dead bodies. For example, we had a story about a fisherman being washed off rocks and his body was later found. We got shots of the rocks that illustrated the danger of the area. We hadn't shown dead bodies before, so we just got a very long distance shot of what looked like a body with people around it. That was a fairly graphic one. I also remember the horrific fires we had in 1969, when seven people were burnt to death on the Geelong–Melbourne Road. We had shots of the bodies trapped on the fence near Lara. We didn't show those, but we did use the fire brigade staff to say that those who died did the wrong thing. They should have stayed in their cars. That was the message they were trying to give all the time: 'Don't get out of your car! Stay in it, and you've got a chance of surviving. If you get out of the car, there's no way you're going to survive.'

One of the things we had a long discussion about was when the South Vietnamese general shot a girl through the head in Saigon. This was right in the middle of the Vietnam War. We actually even talked to our commercial rivals about how we were going to tackle it. I remember various news editors agreeing that yes, they would show the shot and we did. We had more time to handle major stories from overseas. We were able to get a better understanding of the story, I suppose, when the pictures came in. We had time to look at it, time to think about it, because by the time we got any film from overseas it was 12 hours or a day old and our viewers would have already read or heard about it. Actually you get fairly shock-proof after a while.

We also had to be careful about court reports. These days you've still got to be wary of showing people's faces. In those days, you couldn't block the faces out especially when people were being filmed moving around. Again, this is one of the experiments we devised and rehearsed. I don't know how they did it technically, but the graphics people superimposed a black mask across the face of the person who was moving. They rehearsed it a few times so they knew just which way to get it to move too. They didn't practice many times, I might add, because of the time involved. The technician sat in front of that film to monitor the action so that he could follow the film and the person's face all the time.

BEING A JOURNALIST

Getting the story across and finding the best way of doing it were my two main motivators as a journalist and news producer. Working under pressure, you don't have too much time to think about the best way to deal with everything as it comes, but later you think, 'We could do that better, so next time I'll try it this way and see how we go'.

We were lucky at ABV2 because when we were on the sub-editing desk we used to have a long lunch at the Elsternwick Hotel, the 'Big E'. There we were able to sit down and talk about how we could do things and people would throw around ideas. The chief sub-editor might be there, and some of the junior ones too, and we were all able to talk in that informal atmosphere and come up with ideas that we could try out. It wasn't officially work, it was our lunch hour, except that, shall we say, the lunch hour extended into working time. We were working, we were talking shop. It *was* a good idea. I think that when people get a bit toey about going out for long lunches with your colleagues, sometimes you can lose some valuable ideas that get thrown around (especially after several glasses of red wine – you become more creative). It was a good way to relax too.

We also had to get along with each other. You wouldn't be able to do this work unless you did get on well. We were working under a very tight deadline, putting on an unrehearsed half-hour show and we had to respect each other's abilities and disabilities. We were also working under pressure in a confined area, although the offices weren't small, you just had to get on with people. If people found the pressure too much they went back to radio.

That was the interesting part of this time period, from 1964 to 1968. Prior to that, the ABC was very conservative about their news. It was basically radio news read by someone with a camera. At one stage, I was told the news was limited to three 30-second films or something like that per bulletin. By the time I arrived at ABV2, the hierarchy was a bit more relaxed about what we're doing and how we were using all sorts of different ideas to improve the television news coverage.

In those four years we were trying things out, developing news, and learning more about television news and what you could do. We had a very good news editor. He was getting near to retirement and he didn't want to know a thing about television. He just said, 'I'll back you up, whatever you do.' I think that was one of my favourite periods of my working life, because we had the freedom to experiment. Head Office in Sydney was pretty relaxed; if we got away with one of our experiments, it was, 'Oh, good work, good work, chaps', and if we mucked things up, 'Oh, it's only Melbourne'.

Travel across australia

I had well and truly been bitten by the travel bug, and the six weeks' annual leave gave me the chance to see some of Australia. In the winter of 1965, I travelled for five weeks through central and northern Australia. The trips on The Ghan, Sunlander and Inlander trains were memorable ones. I went as far north as Darwin that time.

On my next trip, I think I used every possible mode of transport. I took a series of trains from Melbourne to Perth via Adelaide, and drove around the Perth area for a bit. Then I took a ship, the *MV Kabbarli*, a WA state government ship used for coastal shipping, from Fremantle all the way up the coast to Wyndham.

Casuarina Beach, Darwin, 1966

While the ship was being serviced and we were waiting until we could leave at high tide, I took a day trip by coach to Kununurra about 100 kilometres southeast of Wyndham to see the new Ord River Scheme. I continued by the same ship to Darwin. At the end of my trip, I flew home on TAA, Trans-Australia Airlines (government-owned, eventually becoming Qantas Domestic).

It was two years later, at the end of my time at ABV2, before I next went off travelling.

Chapter Seven

AROUND THE WORLD IN NINE MONTHS

In 1967, I was working in the news department for the ABC in Melbourne, and seeing a lot of foreign news come in. This was a pretty interesting time: there had been a military coup in Greece and the King had gone into exile, Che Guavera was killed in Bolivia, and the Six-Day War had taken place in the Middle East. I was lying in bed one night thinking, 'I haven't been overseas and I'm 31 years old. I've got to do something about this.' So almost immediately I went to the travel agent and booked – a year in advance – a passage on the *Patris*, a ship of the Chandris line, to go to Europe.

PREPARATIONS AND PLANNING

I started saving madly, and even sold the car to raise enough money to go around the world. I booked early, and told people I was going, to make sure I couldn't change my mind and back out. I even started learning German from a German–English phrasebook on my long Chief of Staff shifts on Sundays, when usually very little happened in the newsroom but someone had to be there in case something did. I worked out that the Germans had been around most of Europe, whether they were wanted there or not, so there was a good chance most people could speak German or some sort of German. I taught myself basic tourist phrases and limited conversation that was certainly enough to buy railway tickets, order meals and get a bed and breakfast.

I had asked my news editor for six months' leave without pay commencing in April 1968. He regretted that he wasn't able to give me the leave at that time. So I said, 'Well, I'm off anyway,' and I resigned. I gave the ABC three months' notice and gave myself the opportunity to plan a longer trip.

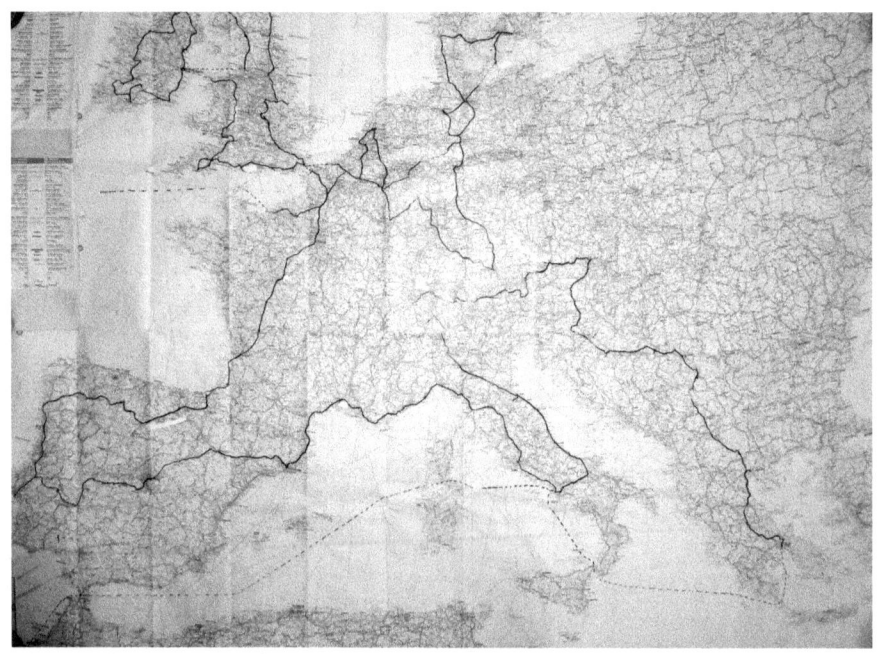

Cliff's map of his world trip, 1968

For several months before I left, I planned all the details of my world trip. As rail was the best and cheapest way to travel, and a station was at the centre of every city and town, I got out a map of Europe and studied all the train lines. I worked out all the distances and the routes, and the things that I wanted to see, and planned my itinerary from that. My route started in Greece, where the ship berthed at Piraeus, went through Yugoslavia to Austria, Liechtenstein,

Switzerland and Italy into France and Spain, to Portugal, back into Spain and France, then to England, Scotland, Ireland and Wales. From there I went across Europe again to Belgium, the Netherlands, Luxembourg, Germany and Denmark, back through Germany, Belgium and France. I returned by ship to Australia, on a different liner, via the United States, the West Indies, Mexico, Canada, Hawaii, Fiji, and New Zealand – twenty-five countries in nine months. I wanted to include everything!

ABOARD THE *PATRIS*

I left Melbourne on the return trip of an assisted migrant voyage ship, the *Patris*, on 21 April 1968. We had to travel via the Cape of Good Hope because the Suez Canal was still filled with sunken ships from the Six-Day War in 1967. So we didn't go via Columbo – we went from Sydney to Adelaide, Fremantle, around the Cape to Cape Town, then through the South and North Atlantic to Gibraltar, and then on to Greece.

The Patris, circa *1968*

It was an interesting little sojourn on the Indian Ocean. We had our first fire drill and the announcements were initially made in both Greek and English. On this occasion, the English-speaking people were told to go to one of the lounges, so we dutifully went there. From then on, all the announcements were in Greek only, and we saw the Greek-speaking passengers going to their lifeboats. Suddenly, a very harassed senior officer came in, asking us in Greek why we hadn't gone to our lifeboats. We explained to him in English that we couldn't understand a word that was being said. He apologized profusely and gave us directions in English. There were only a hundred English speakers and 800 Greek expats on board. For the whole time of the voyage, about five weeks, I took the opportunity to have Greek lessons every day. So by the time I got there, I was able to speak a little bit of Greek which was a bonus.

I had a lower bunk in a four-berth cabin with three other men. Across the corridor was a shower block and toilet block. It was very basic accommodation, but the fare was very cheap! We had a day to see the sights in Cape Town, and my cabin mates and I went for a look around together. At the end of the day, I still had some South African rand left (worthless anywhere else) and we decided to spend it on the local Castle beer in a pub at the port. Suddenly we realised that we had one minute before our ship sailed, and ran for it. There was just one gangplank left in position, which went straight to the crew's quarters, so we bundled ourselves on board there just in time. This was good training for the European railway system, which, with few exceptions, is very punctual.

The next port was Gibraltar where I managed to see one of the famous apes, and drink a bit of warm beer. The English in Gibraltar are more English than the English, and strangely don't chill their beer even though they are living almost on the equator.

In the next port, Naples, I had a quick lesson on my tourist dress code. I had dressed up in tailored trousers and a nice sports coat. Between the gangplank and the gate, I endured practically every expensive inducement to part with my money. In contrast, one of my cabin mates, much more sensibly dressed in a dirty old pair of jeans, was offered special deals on goods for the crew! We usually stopped in port for about twelve hours, just long enough for us to have a look around, and for the crew to get new provisions on board. This time, Greek immigration officials from Naples also came on board. They were there to go through the passenger lists to make sure that there was no one on board who was hostile to the Greek colonels – the military junta. There were five engineers on board. Now, I knew the ship only needed four. The alleged fifth engineer knew that I was a journalist and, every now and again during the voyage, I was invited to his cabin along with other people for Metaxa brandy and other drinks. I had my suspicions about this bloke, who at 3.00 am kept asking me in-depth questions about the political situation in Greece. Luckily I had enough sense to say that whatever the Greeks did was their business, not mine. I found it was always wise to be diplomatic when pressed for my opinion on the affairs of host countries. He finally revealed himself when the passengers were being checked through immigration. He was standing behind the immigration officers and giving the thumbs up or thumbs down. They looked at me a little bit, then turned to him and he indicated that I was OK, so I disembarked at Piraeus.

Heading north through Europe

We were able to stay on the *Patris* in Piraeus for two days, enabling me to see Athens and then set off to start the first part of my train trip heading north through Larissa and then Thessaloniki, then across Europe to the United Kingdom. It was time to put my detailed plans into effect.

Generally, I would arrive in a new location in the morning, book into a budget hotel near the station and then spend the rest of the day roving around the town and taking photos of the main tourist attractions. I'd stay overnight, then get on a train in time to arrive at the next place around mid-morning. I had worked it out that I only needed to travel for an hour or so to most destinations, so I would have pretty well all day to spend in one place. When I arrived in a new place, I would check the next day's train departure times for the onward trip. I thought I was pretty well organised.

As I was on a very tight budget, my usual procedure was to look for a cheap-looking hotel that didn't have a doorman or other trappings of expense. I'd ask for a room, and give them my limit in the local currency. Often they would manage to find a little room, usually next to the toilets, that was within my budget. I always chose hotels near the station, so that I didn't have to carry my suitcase too far and knowing that, in the smaller towns at least, most of the attractions would be within walking distance.

About the only time my usual approach didn't work was in Belgrade, Yugoslavia as it was then. It was the first Communist country I'd been to, and it was drab. The people didn't seem very helpful or cheerful and it wasn't a good start. I had a Serbo-Croat-English phrasebook which basically got me a feed, but when I tried to get accommodation in a tourist hotel in Belgrade, they sent me away. One doorman looked as though he was some former senior administrator who had been given this lacklustre job after the Communists had taken over. As I still had found nowhere to sleep by 11.00 that night, I went back to the railway station and waited for the next train to Austria, which was at about 5.00 am. I slept, or sat and dozed, on a seat on the platform. The guard tried to shift me along a couple of times, but he couldn't speak English, and I couldn't speak any Serbo-Croat. Luckily it was the beginning of summer, so it wasn't very cold. This was one of the very few times my travels did not go to plan. I also dropped the idea of going on to a resort on the Adriatic coast, which was too difficult to get to, and moved on to Austria.

In contrast to my adventure in Belgrade, I was glad to be able to book straight into a suitable hotel in Vienna. I got settled, and wandered off for something to eat. It was a warm night in early summer, and as I was walking in one of the central parks, I first heard and then saw, right in front of me, a full orchestra playing Strauss waltzes in the open air. It was beautiful and it was free for whoever wanted to walk in and listen. I still remember that night very clearly. It was just magic.

Switzerland and Liechtenstein

My rail-based route often took me off the more established tourist track. After Linz and Salzburg, I took a slow train rather than an express through the Tyrol to Innsbruck, westward towards Switzerland. I remember the conductor saying, 'Oh, if you get off now there'll be a big express that'll take you right through.' I said, 'Look, I'm quite happy to stop every now and again. I've got tons of time.' Eventually it got to the point where he'd say, 'Five minutes here, you go and have a look. I'll wait for you.' So I got a chance to see some of the little villages in the beautiful Tyrol Valley. It's a magical place. Innsbruck is a beautiful town; the mountains towering above it are still capped with snow even in summer.

In Liechtenstein I stopped at Schaan, the only railway station in the tiny principality. I stayed at a little hotel there near the station. Schaan is only about 4 or 5 kilometres from the capital Vaduz, which has a picture-book royal castle. From Vaduz, I walked to Balzers where I found a beer festival: a big tent, two bands playing – modern rock and German drinking songs – and big steins of beer being served. There were stalls selling German-style food. By then I could speak a little German and I had a delightful time. Then Princess Georgina, the wife of the Crown Prince, arrived to officially open the festival. She came with just a driver, no security or anything like that, and there was only one policeman on duty at the festival. She opened the car door herself, saluted, waved to the people, and chatted with them. Everyone stood up as the Liechtenstein national anthem was played (to the same tune as 'God Save the Queen'). It was an extraordinary moment.

As an extra adventure, I decided I'd take the Royal Liechtenstein Mail bus to Malbun, the most eastern part of Liechtenstein. The bus had right of way on all these roads which, generally speaking, are only one car width wide. Inevitably, coming around a corner, we encountered an Italian tourist bus coming the other way. It had to reverse to the nearest passing point, since it had to give way. As it was reversing, it backed into a car driven by a German tourist. Luckily no one was travelling very fast! The Italian bus driver got out and started talking to the German driver.

Meanwhile, the driver with the Royal Liechtenstein Mail turned his engine off, got his newspaper out, and started to read it. Obviously it wasn't the first time this situation had occurred. He knew exactly what to do: wait until it was all sorted out, then resume his regal, right-of-way route with the mail. We got to Malbun, and I took the chairlift right to the top. From there was I was able to see into Yugoslavia, Austria and Liechtenstein itself. I was pleased that I had discovered the mail bus; even without a commentary, it was much better that the tourist options. Also, since I always checked the tourist information available at each station to see what options were available, I knew I couldn't afford a tour.

I took the train to Zurich, and while in Switzerland I also went to Bern to see the famous bears and to visit the Universal Postal Union statue. This was one of the important things that that I had planned to visit before I left Australia. The statue commemorates the founding of the Universal Postal Union in 1874. It shows five messengers representing the five continents, as they pass letters around the globe. This statue appears on many stamps, several of which I was pleased to have in my collection. Being a philatelist from a young age, I was very interested to see the real thing and I was not disappointed.

Universal Postal Union Monument, Berne, June 1968

A Republic of Guinea stamp showing the UPU Monument

Italy and San Marino

En route to Italy, I took the train south from Bern through the Simplon tunnel, which connects Brig in Switzerland with Domodossola in Italy. From there the train goes to Milan. The tunnel is straight except for very tight curves at either end, but it descends very steeply which was pretty alarming but well worth it when you emerge to enjoy the most spectacular view of the Italian countryside.

From Milan I set off for Bologna, and from there to the east coast of Italy. I took a local bus to the delightful Republic of San Marino, a tiny sovereign state of only 62 square kilometres surrounded by Italy. Independent for about 1000 years, it is one of those places which is three-quarters sheer cliffs. The town is on top of an escarpment which slopes down the other side. Anyone wanting to invade would have only one very dangerous way to approach, and it would not be worth the trouble. There are three lookout towers on the cliffs that were built hundreds of years ago and were featured on San Marino stamps.

San Marino towers, June 1968

Notably, also, I fell in love with a Finnish bus driver there, and I remember sitting on the escarpment drinking San Marino brandy with him, looking out onto the vista on the clearest of days. Bus drivers were allowed to drink then! We ended up going back to his place, and after a very pleasant evening, I got the trolley bus back to the guest house I had booked at Rimini on the coast. There I was met by a most irate porter who had waited up for my return. I didn't know he was going to do that.

A funny thing happened on the way to Foggia, my next destination. I was in a compartment with seven others, all chaps with five o'clock shadows and dark features. One spoke to me in very broken English (but by that time I could speak a little bit of Italian). He noticed one of my suitcases with its Australian label, and asked, 'Australian?' I said, 'Si.' He said to me, 'Cousin in Sydney, you know Sydney? Yes, you know my cousin.' It turns out this is quite something to an Italian, that I'm from Australia and he's got a cousin in Sydney. Next thing I know, a very vicious-looking knife comes out, and then pieces of bread and some unknown pre-cooked meat. He makes me a sandwich and everyone has big smiles on their faces. So with a big smile on my face, I accepted.

From there I went west to Naples. Dressed in old jeans and a shirt, this time I was rarely accosted for money. I had learned my lesson! I visited all the usual tourist attractions, and saw some of the less visited parts of the city. I had also learnt to be extra cautious in these areas and was very discreet taking photos so that I wouldn't have my camera stolen. I always carried a little travel bag with my passport, money and the camera, and I never carried much cash. In those days, credit cards were pretty unusual. I'd usually only change as much money as I needed into the local currency, and spend it all before I left the country. In those days Australian currency wasn't convertible, it was a fixed currency. You could change Australian dollars in England, but not in European countries. I kept five American dollars in dollar notes to change if I needed local cash. Everyone was happy to change

American dollars. Whether they gave me the right amount of local money for them or not, I don't know. I was very careful with cash because I didn't have any to spare. I had to eat in local restaurants that had their menus and prices on the windows, so that I knew I could afford to eat there. When you're hungry, and there's no-one around who speaks English, you learn a language very fast, and I got quite good at reading menus in foreign languages.

The next stops were Rome and Florence, and from there on to Pisa. I enjoyed all the main sights and was fortunate enough to be able to climb to the top of the Leaning Tower, and walk around the balcony at the top. It was a bit eerie; there were no guard rails on the balcony, and the Tower does really lean. The Cathedral of Pisa is right next to the Tower. Pisa is a walled city, and not much changes inside the walls. I returned thirty years later to find it looked very much the same.

I took the train from Pisa to Genoa which runs along the Ligurian coast, and there are about fifty tunnels and twenty bridges on the way. When you come out of one of those tunnels through the cliffs, you see lovely little villages and beautiful beaches. It was such a fantastic journey I went back there with Rob many years later to take that train trip again.

At Monte Carlo again I did the usual tourist things. Prince Rainier and Princess Grace were in residence at the time, but I didn't see them. Looking at the wealth everywhere – the yachts in the harbour, and the millionaire's cars – I thought that I could have been a gigolo if I was a bit younger. I moved on to Nice, where the beaches are made of pebbles, and I couldn't understand why people would lie down on them! Getting off the train in Nice, the handle came off my suitcase, and I had to heave it along the road. Luckily it had a strap around it, and, as always, there was a cheap little hotel near the station. I bought myself two small suitcases so that I was neatly balanced when I left for Marseilles. This worked so well I have carried two suitcases or travel bags ever since.

I reached Montpellier on Bastille Day, which was fun. The streets next to my hotel were barricaded for the celebration and there was a concert in the town square with stalls selling food and drink. It was a big night. I had just got to bed when, at about 4.00 am, some happy Montpellien drove his car into the barricade, creating a great uproar. I imagine that the way the locals were drinking, he probably couldn't see the barricade, and he may have not even known he was driving his car!

From Montpellier I travelled south to Barcelona in Spain, changing from French standard gauge to Spanish broad gauge railway on the way. The train arrived late and I didn't see too much there before moving on to Zaragoza. As Spanish trains tended to do in those days, that train was running six hours late, and then we were stuck for about three or four hours in the middle of nowhere. There was a woman with three children in my compartment, peeling and eating boiled eggs. In the heat, without air conditioning, this produced a powerful stench. It was a great relief to get the windows open when we got moving again.

I finally got to Zaragoza much later in the day than I intended, at about 10.00 pm. Sometimes, there would be people at the station who offered a private bed and breakfast arrangement in their own homes, I suppose as a way of making a bit of extra money. A bloke at the Zaragoza station offered me this kind of arrangement for a very cheap price. Somewhat nervously I accepted, and followed him through back streets until we got to his place. A woman came out to the front, and asked, 'Passport, please.' I showed it to her and, exclaiming 'Australian, Australian, Australian!', she disappeared.

Next, a very pregnant young lady comes out and I thought to myself, 'God, what did the last Australian do here?' She says, 'G'day mate, how are you?' She was a girl from Sydney, the daughter-in-law of the owners, and had married a Spaniard while he was studying in Australia. The couple had decided to return to Spain to have the baby because the baby could then get dual citizenship. She was homesick for Australia, so we chatted till the wee hours of the morning. We had a marvellous time. In the morning we had a traditional breakfast of goat's milk, fruit, bread and a cup of coffee, and the landlord showed me the way back to the station for my next train.

THE UNITED KINGDOM

After another week in Spain and Portugal and three days of wonderful sightseeing in Paris, I headed to England. I took the train to Calais, and got the ferry across to Dover. I met a Canadian soldier on the ferry, and we drank a lot of beer together. I wasn't quite sober when I arrived in Dover, but we got through immigration very fast – I think the authorities just wanted to get rid of us. I was delighted to be able to speak English again, though I wasn't sure that they actually spoke English in London!

I stayed for four days with a penfriend who I had been writing to for four or five years, which saved a lot of money. He lived in inner London, very handy, and it was good to meet him in person. We talked about what we'd written to one another, and every day he went to work and I went out to look around. I took in all the usual tourist spots – Tower Bridge, Buckingham Palace, St Paul's Cathedral, the Tower of London, the Thames, Marble Arch, Piccadilly Circus, and the Houses of Parliament. I went often on the double-decker buses. The view from upstairs was fantastic, and I could get a day ticket.

I took a tour of the BBC studios, and my guide took me on the set of 'Z Cars', a very popular police TV serial. Unfortunately, it was one of those days where everything was going wrong and the producer was not only tearing her hair out but tearing everyone else's hair out as well! We, two innocent people, walked in the door, and immediately copped a blast. So we didn't linger.

While in the UK, I visited a friend of my mother's in Foston. Mum had met her when she travelled in England with a couple of her nursing colleagues in 1956. The friend, Mrs Brieant, lived in a little sixteenth-century stone cottage. She was a short lady and had no problem, but

I kept hitting my head on the door frames because the doors were built for very short people in the sixteenth century. She made her own lovely wine from vegetables – parsnips, turnips, carrots – and one afternoon we tried a few of them. She was in her sixties in those days, bright as anything. After a few glasses of this wine, I was holding myself up on the walls, because I didn't have too much alcohol when I was travelling (I couldn't afford it). So I got tipsy fairly quickly.

Another highlight of the trip was my time in Edinburgh. I was there for the Edinburgh Festival, and arrived in time to see the Military Tattoo in the Palace Forecourt of Edinburgh Castle. There are stands for spectators on each side of the Forecourt, and it's a magnificent spectacle as the performers march through the gates of the castle. It was a fine, dry night too. Another high spot, literally, was on the walls of Edinburgh Castle where I was taking some photos. The castle overlooks the valley of the Leith, the river that runs through Edinburgh, and Princes Street (the main street) and the railway station are in this valley. Looking down from the castle, I saw massed pipe bands marching along the street. When you hear pipe bands, the further away you are, the better they sound.

Princes Street, Edinburgh, June 1968

I arrived in Aberdeen on 22 August 1968, just after the invasion of Prague by Soviet troops. The Prague Spring was a democratic uprising that was crushed in a pretty brutal fashion. All day, RAF fighter jets flew up and down the east coast of England and Scotland and out into the North Sea, on stand-by in case things escalated out of control. It was an interesting time. Although I didn't get much chance to keep up with all the news, I did hear that twenty journalists and other staff were killed at Radio Prague because they would not stop broadcasting. Sometimes there would be a TV in the hotel lounge, and now and again I would see the local paper. Of course, if I was in Europe, neither of these were much good to me since the news would be in the local language.

Ireland

Continuing my travels, I went to Ireland. I had the opportunity to visit RTÉ, Radio and Television Ireland, in Dublin. I was in Northern Ireland in September 1968. The IRA hadn't started bombing and killing people at that stage, nor were the Protestants retaliating, but you could feel the tension there. I was travelling on a local bus from Sligo to Enniskillen. Two border guards got on the bus at the border when we stopped. They didn't ask for my passport, but they examined the bus; that is, they walked the length of the bus, looked under the back seat, and walked back. So they were pretty relaxed. Then I went on to Londonderry where the tension was unmistakable. Every time I went into a pub for a drink I brought it to a standstill. 'Are you one of us, or are you a Mick?' or, 'Are you one of us, or a Proddy?' I would reply, 'Don't know, mate, I'm Australian. I'd like a beer.' And the response would be, 'Oh, no worries. He's Australian, he's okay.'

In Belfast I took my usual tourist wander, and walked up a rocky hill in one of the city parks. I thought I would get good shots of the city from up there. Winding up the hill through shrubs and trees, I came to a clearing right near the top. There were four people doing target practice with pistols – not the shots I was expecting! I thought to myself, 'Cliff, this is something you didn't see.' This is a moment where you become very discreet, quietly turn around 180 degrees, tiptoe away, and don't look back. I had learnt to obey my sixth sense for danger and would back out quickly when my alarm bells went off. They kept on firing their pistols, so obviously they hadn't seen me. I think they were preparing for the conflict that ensued the following year.

Back to Europe

In hindsight, I am astonished that I managed to see so much during my first overseas trip. After Ireland, I caught the ferry to Wales and travelled around the beautiful south of England. I took the Dover ferry back across the Channel to Belgium and stayed at Ghent, Brussels and Antwerp, followed by Rotterdam, The Hague and Amsterdam in the Netherlands.

In Amsterdam I was amazed to see the material displayed in the shop windows of adult bookstores; a range of magazines that you would never, ever see in Australia. No bland brown paper covers either! It was all full frontal, and I remember looking at them open-mouthed, then having a terrible guilty feeling of, 'What if one of my relatives came along and saw me staring at all these things?' The locals were completely unconcerned; the Dutch had relaxed their censorship laws at some time in the 1950s.

While I was still at work in Australia, I'd also made an appointment to visit Radio Netherlands at Eindhoven. I'd written to them, and they had offered to show me around. I had a very nice tour of the exceptionally up-to-date facilities of Radio Netherlands and was also taken out for a very tasty vegetarian lunch. It was all very enjoyable.

After two weeks touring Luxembourg and Germany, I headed to Denmark, the most northerly destination of my trip. I had to take the bus from Hirschberg in Germany to the border because the railway tracks had been torn up after the war on the German side – the railway had been used to supply the invasion force into Denmark. After great interest had been shown in my Australian passport by the border police, I had missed the train – an extremely rare occurrence for me. The next train was filled with school children and, for about an hour before the next stop, I was giving English lessons to a carriage full of Danish children. It was quite good fun really.

By now it was early November, and I was mentally very tired from the continual travelling. It was also very cold, 4° C. In Copenhagen I had to wear all my clothes at the same time, in layers, since I had no European-type clothes to combat the cold, and no money to buy any. Pushing onwards, I made my way back through Germany and Belgium to Le Havre, in France, where I was to board the *Orsova* for the voyage home to Australia via the Atlantic this time. That was a P & O ship – a proper passenger liner. I had cashed in my return ticket on the Chandris line because I didn't want to return on a migrant ship, and had to pay extra for the ticket on the *Orsova*. I had earlier written to my mother and said, 'If you ever want to see your loving son again, you better send him some money', which she did, at 5 per cent interest. Mum taught me a lot about handling money! Before departing on 14 November 1968, I also sent a letter to my dear old ABC TV editor to see if I might be re-employed on my return.

Crossing the Atlantic and home

Having spent hardly more than two days in the one place for six months, it took several days of rest and relaxation at sea for my tourist appetite to return, but it did. After crossing the Atlantic, we stopped at several ports in Bermuda, Fort Lauderdale and Miami Beach in the United States and Nassau in the Bahamas before sailing through the Panama Canal.

When the ship docked at Acapulco in Mexico, one of the cabin staff told us where to get very cheap tequila – half the price – and one of the passengers that I'd gotten to know was leaving the ship at San Francisco. He wanted a dozen, so we bought those, and one extra as a gift for the cabin boy. In San Francisco, we had a few days in port, so this chap invited a group of passengers to his house. He was not allowed to bring more than one bottle of tequila into the country. He took one; the other eleven bottles came with the rest of us in our overnight bags. We just walked through customs, waving our ship passes.

He and his boyfriend picked me up the next evening, and we toured around a number of gay nightclubs. Eventually we finished up at one where I met another young man, who was from San Jose. I didn't go back to my ship that night. When I came back to the *Orsova* the next morning for breakfast, still wearing the clothes I had on from the previous night, some people had a bit of a chat about that.

Everywhere I went, including that evening, I souvenired a matchbook or small box of matches, which was a common way of advertising the restaurant, club or bar you were visiting. I gave all these to my mother for her match collection. She didn't know it, but she had a whole range of gay nightclub matches in her collection.

The Orsova *at Port Everglades, Florida, November 1968*

On the way from Vancouver to Hawaii, we ran into a ferocious North Pacific storm. The crew had strung ropes on the corridors for people to hang on to, and everyone was taking seasickness tablets. The worst part was having lunch served by green-faced stewards. I thought I might go upstairs on the deck and have a look, so I climbed up the stairs, pulled myself along the deck and got near the bow of the ship just in time to see the bow going underneath a huge wave. I thought, 'I don't think I really wanted to see that after all', and retired inside.

Finally, the ship arrived in Sydney, and I was glad to be back in Australia. I was exhausted. I took the overnight train back to Melbourne. I had just enough for a first-class sleeper, and just enough for the train from Melbourne to Geelong. Dad collected me at the station. I think I got home with about five cents to my name.

Mum and Dad were pleased to see me back safe and sound. I think Mum might have worried about me from time to time, but I sent her a postcard every single day for the whole length of the trip. It was fairly easy to get the postcards, and often they were free at tourist information booths. There were plenty of places to buy stamps; sometimes you could even buy them at the station. Mum kept that collection of postcards, and I still have them.

That trip was a magnificent nine months. It opened my eyes to the way the rest of the world does things, and broadened my outlook on life. It was such a success, it whetted my appetite and firmly established my lifelong love for and obsession with travel.

Chapter Eight

THE TAPE AGE – TV AND RADIO

RETURNING TO ABC TELEVISION

I was very happy to rejoin ABV2 in early January 1969 and start earning money again. I had no car and no accommodation so I quickly found a flat in Chaucer Street, St Kilda, which was cheap and close to the ABC. After gallivanting around the world, inevitably, I came down to earth with a thud. My colleagues at Channel 2 had barely noticed my absence – 'Oh Cliff, been away on holidays, have you?' I hadn't been there for nearly a year!

I resumed my previous roles doing chief of staffing, sub-editing and producing the news. We were getting into the humdrum of running just a normal news service, although we never called a news service 'normal'. It wasn't long before I started looking around again. However, I was enjoying saving and was doing as much overtime and extra work as I could; I even tried being a waiter very briefly. I didn't do much travelling that year but I did do a bit of bushwalking and hiking, and even a couple of overnight camping trips with my friend Linton Spencer when I could get away at the weekend.

Then an offer came that I couldn't refuse – more money and a promotion. It came from Channel O, which is now Channel 10. I decided in a flash to take it and off I went. I gave ABV2 the minimum notice, bought a car (Channel O was in Nunawading), and even managed two weeks' holiday – a solo road trip from Geelong, Portland to Mount Gambier and back. This was the first of many road and camping trips I took in the Renault 10, either by myself or with friends around Victoria, and to New South Wales, North Queensland and South Australia, over the next five years.

Renault 10, Carnarvon National Park, Queensland, June 1971

CHASING THE NEWS AT CHANNEL O

I joined Channel O on 16 February 1970 as an 'A' grade journalist in the Chief of Staff position. The promotion was very welcome. I was already back on my feet but I was glad to further increase my saving capacity. It also allowed me to buy my first unit, a flat in Irving Avenue, Windsor, which I purchased 'off the plan'. Coming from the ABC newsroom, however, I did experience a bit of a 'commercial' culture shock – one which ultimately resulted in my 'resignation' two years later.

Unfortunately, their idea of news and my idea of news were not quite consistent. I was looking to produce a more serious style of

17 Irving Avenue, Windsor, February 1973

news. It was like the comparison between *The Age* and the tabloid ambulance-chaser *The Herald-Sun* in newspapers. Channel O news editors were most keen on disasters, or if someone got themselves into trouble, and that type of sensational stuff. Fires or accidents with good pictures were priority stories. I wanted to cover more serious topics – political, cultural and development stories that went slightly beyond the ambulance-chasing – the real news.

We did have a news editor – I think he was more PR than news – but he wasn't very good at explaining what he had in mind. As Chief of Staff, I would be there early in the mornings and have things worked out, and by the time he came in at 8.00 or 9.00 am all of the day was already planned. Often, in the aftermath of a more dramatic event occurring later in the day, the question would be asked, 'Why didn't we cover such and such?' If it was a news story, we would have, but usually it was because I didn't know anything about it! Occasionally, I went out reporting and someone else came in as Chief of Staff. They frequently made a bigger mess than I did, and then I would be back again. Nevertheless, I did have a lot of fun 'chasing' the news.

One of the more spectacular events we covered was the first Vietnam War Moratorium in Melbourne in May 1970. We were expecting a huge crowd to come into the city, estimated to be over 100,000 people. I had to work out how to cover this event knowing that my camera crews couldn't move around very much among so many people. So I only put a couple on the ground and told them

View of Vietnam Moratorium March, Melbourne, May 1970. The cameramen can be seen on the roof of the verandas in the foreground.

The tape age – TV and radio

to do what they could without getting trampled. Then I went to the Sales Manager and I asked, 'What sponsors have we got with stores on Bourke Street?' He said, 'Prouds is one of our sponsors'. I told the Sales Manager to tell Prouds that we wanted to put a camera crew up on their veranda! It was opposite Myer and we got a fantastic shot of the whole of Bourke Street from Parliament House, right down to Elizabeth Street and on to Queen Street. It was an ideal spot; we had brilliant pictures.

To anticipate the news, I would listen to the police radio which you weren't supposed to do in those days. Police liaison with the media wasn't very good, so in this way we would get their news as it was happening. This was a particularly good way of reporting on bank robberies which were more prevalent in the days before there were proper anti-theft devices like pop-up screens. For example, one day I heard a report and had a camera crew and journalist in the vicinity. On a two-way radio I asked one, 'Are you in Brighton Road near the Commonwealth Bank?' He said, 'Yeah, I can see the Commonwealth Bank.' I said, 'It's being robbed at the moment. *Don't* go in! Wait till the police arrive, then go and ask them what they are doing.' Sure enough, a couple of sirens were heard, and police cars soon turned up, and our crew was right on the spot. It was one of those 'accidental' things. I didn't want the crew barging in before the police arrived because they would want to know how we knew!

I had the police radio going on a fairly low volume all the time behind me. You could tell by the sound of their voices whether something was happening or not. They used codes. Signal 33 was a dead body. Signal 30 was a drunk. There was a whole range for robberies, car accidents and whatever. I had the list of codes in front of me so I just listened. I would note, 'Okay, it's only a drunk, only a minor car accident, no need to call the ambulance, only a "bingle", don't worry about it.' The police themselves would get very excited; they were happy that their boredom was being relieved as well.

THE WESTGATE BRIDGE DISASTER

One day, I was at Tullamarine interviewing ballet dancer Garth Welsh who had just returned from an overseas tour – one of those padding stories – when we got a call that the partly constructed Westgate Bridge had fallen down. We had to get there as quickly as we could, and we did. I was one of the first reporters on the scene. I also had Alan Weatherly, the cameraman, a very nice meek gentleman and a very good cameraman, and his young assistant with me. The assistant said, 'I'll drive,' and Alan said, 'No, I'll drive.' We got there in 25 minutes! I won't say how many road rules he broke, but we got there. Alan knew what he could get away with and the best way of getting there. That's an example of where a padding story never makes it to air for very obvious reasons.

They were still dragging the bodies out of the water below when we arrived. It was very frightening. One span of the bridge had fallen down, and we were told to keep an eye on another span as it could come down as well. Fortunately, it didn't but we were doing our work with one eye in the sky waiting for any sign of further collapse.

Westgate Bridge collapse, 15 October 1970

In these situations, you couldn't afford to think about the danger or respond to the tragedy. You just had to be a step removed. There's no use bursting into tears; it won't help at all. You had to shut it out or you wouldn't last in the job.

Basically, you're there to get the story – you don't think about anything else. You see the victims' bodies, but you just try to find out the facts. You ask: what's happened, how did it happen, why did it happen, where did it happen? You find someone to ask while everyone is running around in circles. It can be difficult as you also have to keep an eye on anything else that may occur. You don't have a set formula. It's best described as play it by ear, or play it as it happens. There's no use in going in with a scripted plan – forget that. The basic thing again is, what happened? How, why, when and where are the four questions you ask.

We got the early footage, which was key, before handing over to Tom Jones, Channel O's top reporter at the time. We headed straight off and took the film to the lab. And they put it on as news flashes throughout the day, interrupting programming to do it which was fairly rare in those days. It could easily be done in commercial television as they could drop an advertisement, often a complimentary one, so we had more scope than the ABC.

Later, as a reporter with the ABC, I remember being bundled out of bed at 3.00 am to join a waiting camera crew. We were off to cover the havoc caused by the flash flooding in Moonee Ponds caused by the Maribyrnong River.

DEBRIEFING AT THE PUB

Generally, after the difficult stories, such as the Westgate disaster, we would go to the pub and have quite a few drinks with colleagues. This is why journalists have a reputation for heavy drinking. You just needed to be there for the companionship more than to talk about it. What's the point of talking about it? You've seen it. It's just been 'a horror day', 'a really busy day', 'I'm glad to put my feet up, 'yeah, have another drink', another sigh. 'Now I'm feeling a lot better. Do you want another one?' 'Yes, thanks!' You do need to wind down. You just can't keep the adrenaline flowing all the time; you've got to get a good night's sleep.

Outside work, I had plenty of time and my social life was good. I had lots of friends to have a drink and go to parties with. We also got away together for weekends and holidays. I did eighteen trips while I was at Channel O, either alone or with friends. We drove and hiked all around Victoria, visiting places like Hanging Rock, Echuca, Ballarat, Mt Macedon, Waratah Bay, Bellarine Peninsula, Phillip Island, Healesville, and interstate as far as Sydney. I had been to so many places, I started 'spinning the map' to choose the next destination. I would shut my eyes, spin a map of Victoria and put a finger down and then I'd go to the town nearest to my finger.

Linton Spencer at Lake Tali Karng, Alpine National Park, Victoria, May 1971

Meanwhile, my sister Lynnette completed her doctorate in agricultural history from Monash University. A few years later, her combined interests in agricultural science and history took her to the University of Reading in the United Kingdom where she established her career.

Cliff with Lynnette after being awarded her Doctor of Philosophy, December 1970

Charles and Lynn with Lynnette at Tullamarine before her departure to England, September 1975

MEETING ROB YOUNG

It was 1 October 1971 at 7.30 pm in the saloon bar of the Prince of Wales Hotel in St Kilda. This young man looked at me, I looked at him, and we got talking. He was a delightful person and we connected immediately. I spent that first night with him, and he hasn't gone home since!

Rob likes to tell the story in a lot more detail and to 'give the actual facts'. He says,

> I was getting a party together to go out after 10 o'clock. We would meet at the pub and when it closed we would get some bottles and the address and off we'd go. On this night Harvey Robinson said to me, 'That's Cliff Peel over there, he is terrific in the cot!' Anyway I was introduced, and I became 'the boarder who wouldn't go home,' who has been there for forty-four years!

Cliff with Seefah at Irving Avenue, 1972, and Rob Young with 'K' the cat at Chambers Winery, Rutherglen, 1979

The first night we stayed at Rob's place and that was a Friday night. I said, 'Well, on Saturday, I'm going to drive to Moulamein in southern New South Wales.' I had spun the map and that was my destination. I thought, 'That's easy, that's a day's drive up and a day's drive back', so I invited him along. Rob jumped at it and off we went. We got to Moulamein and booked into the hotel and booked dinner

The tape age – TV and radio

The hotel at Moulamein

for about 7.00 pm. It was only about 5.30 pm and we were, shall we say, getting to know each other better, when all of a sudden the window blind flew up with a loud bang! Luckily our room was on the first floor but that still brought things to a fairly abrupt halt. It gave us both a very big fright. Anyhow, we got over that, and came home the next day. Rob moved in with me in my little unit in Chaucer Street, St Kilda. The unit was far too small for two people and Rob tells a lot of stories about that. Fortunately, the unit I had bought in Irving Avenue, Windsor, was nearly completed and we moved in on 17 November 1971.

LEAVING CHANNEL O

Meanwhile, things were not improving at Channel O and I could see that the writing was on the wall. I was getting less and less interesting work, and getting a lot of the crappy, dull jobs. Having bought the Windsor unit, I couldn't afford to lose the job, which paid well. It was a big shock to my system when I went to work one day and I was told that my resignation had been accepted! I said,

'Well, look, I haven't resigned actually ...' 'But if you sign this ...' I said, 'I am not going to sign anything! Pardon me a moment, I am going to make a phone call to the AJA.' I was due to go on holiday in a couple of weeks' time. The AJA told me, 'Oh, yes, yes. That is the usual thing with Channel O. Their ratings are down, so they sack most of the staff and keep the management. They'll start all over again. We will have a chat with the managers, don't worry.' So, shall we say, I went on holidays for six weeks. I didn't go back but a fairly generous addition to my pay was made which paid off the second mortgage on the flat.

This was a great outcome except for the fact that I didn't have a job to go to. But at least I got paid and I had some money up my sleeve. I took off in the Renault 10 to South Australia via Ballarat, Ouyen, Mildura, Broken Hill, Adelaide, Port Pirie, Gawler, Victor Harbour, Edenhope, Horsham and back to Melbourne.

Renault 10 in swamp grass, Wyperfeld National Park, north-west Victoria, March 1970

The Tape Age – TV and Radio

Home to the ABC

Although I got a good reference from Channel O and I knew how everything operated, I wasn't interested in joining any other commercial television stations. I thought, 'I'll go back to the ABC, I know the ABC.' So I rang them up and said, 'I am here, you will need me back!' The reply was, 'No, we don't, but we will give you some freelance or casual jobs.' I was still a bit concerned about paying off the unit, and I had met 'His Nibs' by this time, but at least I kept getting freelance work. Then, after calling me in nearly every day for about six weeks, they said, 'Okay, you're back with us now. We have a permanent position for you at your old salary.' So I agreed, and thought I would stay at the ABC until I retired. I wasn't going to leave again – I might not get back for the fourth time.

In 1969, I did a freelance report for the ABC on CSIRO and the Australian dairy industry. In those days the only cheeses on the market were cheddar, more cheddar and cheddar. Big companies were quite happy to import small quantities of 'fancy cheeses' from overseas. I reported on the inaugural meeting of the Cheese Club, a cheese lover's group, which was importing specialty cheeses, such as French Brie, Camembert, Blue Vein and Roquefort, to show members and to encourage the dairy industry to develop a bigger range of local cheeses.

I thought, as did many others, that this was a rather good idea and joined at the next meeting. Various branches of cheese clubs formed around Australia. The establishment of the cheese clubs coincided with the influx of immigrants from Europe in the 1970s, who brought their skills and liking for imported cheeses with them. The question was why Australian industries didn't make speciality cheeses when we had the best primary product – the milk – and the necessary skills. The clubs also proposed that tariffs be lifted.

The Cheese Club was also a social thing. I edited the newsletter for a time, and was also on the committee. Later, I served as the President of the Melbourne branch. Over time, the aims of the club were achieved. Local and imported cheeses had become readily available.

Setting off from East Hawthorn, 1979

Bike riding

One day, it suddenly occurred to me that I should get a bicycle, so I got one. That was great. It was especially good to ride home from work to unwind after a busy day at work. Then I started riding further. One weekend, I hadn't much to do, so I thought, 'I'll go for a bike ride.' It was fun – so much fun that on my next week off, I planned my first of many long bike rides. I got a lift to Albury and then rode along the Murray River to Swan Hill, staying at night in various places, and came back by train. Working on the fact that the Murray River, like all rivers, flowed downhill, I thought the route must be all downhill and shouldn't be too bad. In fact, it was great. It's a great way of seeing the countryside. You just go along. You don't try and rush around or anything like that.

I also did shorter trips. Although visiting wineries was not usually a good idea when riding, I did do four days of wine touring in McLaren Vale with a friend who was a student at a wine college. We stayed in the McLaren Vale Hotel and visited about forty wineries in four days. The first day we saw ten wineries on the eastern side of the valley, riding to the most distant one and gradually making our way back. Then we went south, north and west, so we covered quite a lot of wineries without any backtracking.

I never booked ahead but always got a good reception when I turned up at hotels to have dinner and stay overnight. People were intrigued to think that I would turn up out of nowhere. I was stared at and possibly regarded as a lunatic, but quite harmless of course. People were always happy to chat to me.

I remember once on a particularly hot day getting to Morgan (in South Australia) and chatting to the owner of the hotel after a hot dry ride. We sat down for a chat, and I said, 'Have you got any wines?' He replied, 'Look, I just bought the hotel. I don't know what's in the cellar. So let's go down and have a look.' Right in the corner was a box of Orlando Riesling. He said, 'Oh, I don't know what this is like – it's ten years old.' The cellar at the Morgan Hotel was built in the

18-something or other and it was solid bluestone. It was beautiful, an ideal place to put wines. I said, 'Well, let's open a bottle anyhow.' We sat down and opened the bottle and it was beautifully aged Riesling. 'It's excellent to drink and it's ten years old.' So we opened a second bottle.

On the road near Mount Mary, South Australia, 1979

THE FIRST ABC TAPES EDITOR

I spent about a year back in ABC television news. There had been a few changes, and I wasn't getting anywhere. Some politics were involved which I didn't understand, didn't follow and was not interested in. Then, the news editor, Tony Wells, said, 'I understand you know something about tapes and sound through commercial radio.' I said, 'Yes, I know a bit about that, and I have worked at Channel O where we did quite a bit more tape work than here in television news at the ABC.' He said that they wanted to introduce sound inserts, such as the 30-second grabs, into the radio news, and put them on cassette to allow the news reader to play them during the news. In other words, it meant lining up these little tape recorders which held up to a minute or more of sound. The newsreader could then say, 'Mrs Buggerlugs said this about that', and play the tape, and you would hear Mrs Buggerlugs' voice coming through. Previously, the newsreader read the full fifteen minutes of news without a break. Nowadays, of course, she or he reads the introduction and then a reporter comes up, and tells you the story with the sound inserts. Well, my job was to implement that system for the ABC. In 1974, that was something new. I became the original Tapes Editor at the ABC Radio News in Melbourne.

THE TAPES ROOM

I was given a little area in the news room at Marland House, 570 Bourke Street, which was also at that particular time the location of the Family Court. We were on the 15th floor, the ABC library was on the 16th floor and the Family Court was on the 17th and 18th floors. That gave us an interesting time because there were all these emotional things going on: occasionally you would get in the lift to find a sobbing woman crying on her solicitor's shoulder, or some bloke who's going to kill someone with a solicitor trying to pacify him, not to mention the chap regularly standing outside with placards because the Family Court had allegedly wronged him. It was quite interesting.

The tapes room was a tiny space. We could only fit in three people at most. It was never intended to be a broadcast studio. The ABC was renting the space, and we had to make do with whatever we could get. Actually, they did extend it to double the size, but it was still pretty small. The studios for the two Melbourne ABC radio stations (3LO and 3AR) were located in Broadcast House in Lonsdale Street but the news broadcasts came from that small news studio in Marland House. All the studios were later transferred to the ABC's new home at Southbank Centre in 1995.

There were a lot of problems working in such a cramped space, but there was also the chance to try things out and to experiment. I really enjoyed that type of work and I did that for twelve years. We did a terrific lot of odd things.

Broadcasting newsvoice from Melbourne

Newsvoice was a ten-minute program that we put on local radio at 5.00 pm each night. It was a summary of news and interviews with about five or six items from around Australia. Now it's probably been superseded by the AM and PM program. Normally I sent items from Melbourne to Sydney for inclusion in the program by landline. However, one day there was a strike in Sydney and the producer of News Voice, Andy Niewenhof, who was supporting the strike, had taken his yacht and was sailing somewhere around the harbour. When they called the strike off and everyone went back to work, of course, they couldn't contact him. Suddenly it was problem and I got a frantic call from Sydney, 'Cliff, can you put Newsvoice on from Melbourne?' I said, 'Yes I can! Send me down the stuff.' I was offered a studio at Broadcast House but I said no, because everything would be coming in through the Tapes Room. It would mean taking all the stuff across to Broadcast House two blocks away and going into an unfamiliar studio. They also offered me extra helpers but by the time I got myself, the newsreader Graeme Evans and the technician George Hunt in the room, there was no space for any more people.

They were intrigued to find out how I would do it. I explained that I would use three tape machines: two to put tapes on, one after the other, and one for the announcer standing with the microphone feeding into the tape machine. We would broadcast alternately via the two outlets. So that's what we did – the announcer came in, read the introduction into the microphone, we then played the story tape, and while that was playing we lined up, plugged in and played the next tape and so on. With the microphone off, we could take a tape

The Tape Age – TV and Radio

off one machine, wind on another and tee it all up without worrying about the noise we were making going out on air.

We calculated the length of the tapes and the introductions and used the theme music to make the final adjustment so we could finish right on time. Again, it was all about the precision timing I had learnt at the Vincent School of Broadcasting. We had to concentrate all the time. There was no time to think about anything else; mostly you wouldn't even have time to write a running sheet. You just have to keep it in your mind and go ahead and let it happen. You always knew exactly where you were up to and, of course, you always watched the clock. I used to manage everything when I was reading the news, which I did occasionally on 3LO. There was always an item at the end which I could drop out. Or I could just read two or three pars (paragraphs). You could read three pars that told the story, while the fourth par gave it a bit more interest but could be dropped if time was tight. You also had the weather forecasts. If you listen carefully to the news, you'll know when they're running short of time. The presenter will read at a faster speed and when they have tons of time, he or she will read in a leisurely way to pad it out. You can always tell. It was fun, and very satisfying when the broadcasts were successfully completed.

Later I went to Sydney to see what they were doing there and met the team. They had the most marvellous studio, the whole works, and about half a dozen people worked there. Afterwards, the blokes said, 'How'd you do it?' I said, 'There were three of us', and I explained how it worked. He said, 'You did what? We could never do that up here.' I said, 'No, so I believe.'

I also received some official recognition on this one via an ABC Inter-Office Memo commending us for producing the first Newsvoice from Melbourne in such difficult conditions. These memos were rare, indeed.

Team work

It was a great time in radio news because we did so many new and different things. We were able, again, to try out new techniques and things that had never been used before in that area. I was assisted by some very, very good technical people. Two technicians in particular were standouts – Neil Hobbs, who came in 1980, and George Hunt. They could both manage the pressure of producing live broadcasts in a crowded space. They were also willing to try new methods, keep the work space very tidy and organised the way we liked it, and share some humour even when we were flat out. We collaborated very well together. One day, after returning from a long lunch, George Hunt said, 'Cliff, I've sent that item up to Sydney, edited it, I did an intro for it too. I hope it's all right, but you weren't here.' I said, 'All right.' He was a technician. He wasn't allowed to do journalist work. As a journalist, I wasn't supposed to do technical work either but that never stopped me. We had no demarcation issues in the Tapes Room; we did what we had to and it worked very well.

It was a good working environment in general. I was happy to coach and mentor, as needed, the new staff coming through to get the best out of them. I was at a time in my career where I could offer journalistic support to others and also be at the forefront of adopting new technology which came on line during the 1980s. From manual typewriters and paper transcripts in the 1970s we moved to telex machines and to computers. There was much resistance to the early DOS computers; no Windows then. We also saw a new generation of cadet journalists, including Ian Henderson, Barry Cassidy and Heather Ewart. They all came through the Tapes Room and learnt how to file voice reports, use microphones, play tapes over the phone and that sort of thing.

The Tape Age – TV and Radio

Dealing with the Pressure

Obviously, we all had to be good at working under pressure. The pressure in the Tapes Room was often extreme, especially when it was getting towards the evening bulletin time, or we were still preparing the sound inserts for each bulletin on the hour, and sending material in time for Newsvoice in Sydney. One of the most helpful things I found I could do was talk on the phone and listen to another person at the same time. I could be saying to someone, 'Yes, okay, good, that would be a good one, 30 seconds, yes, that's right'. Then I'd say, 'George, just cut off there.' I could listen to two things at once – it's called multitasking these days – which was quite handy.

The technical processes themselves were quite simple; it was the timing and content that required the most skill. You had to get the right grabs and, if I wasn't sure about anything, I wouldn't put it to air. I would say, 'I want to check that one', or 'I don't like the sound of that one. I haven't got time to do anything about it now.' I would leave it until after the news and I get the news editor in. It didn't happen very often.

I also learned, very early on, a great technique to deal with abusive people who have made up their minds and won't listen. Back in Rockhampton, I was sitting in the Town Clerk's office one day, getting a story. He answered the phone, and got a blast from the caller. Then he said, 'Well, look, Mrs So-and-So, the reason this is going on is ...' And then he just pressed the disconnect button in the phone cradle, cut himself off, and then hung up the receiver. He said, 'We won't hear from her again. You don't hang up while they're talking – you cut yourself off while you're talking. They won't believe that you'd cut yourself off, so they think the phone's just dropped out and they won't bother ringing again.'

It worked for me on many occasions. I would be polite, go on with a bit of a rigmarole and then, halfway through, just cut myself off. During normal news days, you get occasional complaints about some minor thing. I think that people with nothing else to do often picked up the phone to say, 'I don't think it was quite right that you showed a certain scene', or 'You've overdone that'. We'd even get, 'Why did you have that idiot on? He doesn't know what he's talking about!'

Complaints and abuse calls seemed to peak during elections and other large public events. Members of the public ringing up and abusing the staff was so bad during the 1972 election that we wouldn't let our news assistants (women who did the typing) answer any calls. We said, 'Don't you answer it, let them ring until we come back from the studio and we will deal with it.' We shielded them because of the language being used. It was pretty clear that Labor was going to win, and we'd get calls from people calling us left-wing Communists ruining the country – you name it, they threw it at us. The one that sticks in my mind, the absolute best one, was 'left-wing Hitlerite'!

We had to get used to receiving complaints from viewers. I didn't enjoy them but some were impressive. Again the worst ones were during the 1972 Federal election campaign. I remember getting a burst once from a lady who used the most violent language that I've ever heard from a woman. It was about an item aired on the 7.00 pm television news. I was the unfortunate person to pick up the phone to get a blast. Anyhow, eventually I said, 'My name's Cliff Peel. What's yours?' Her response was, 'F— this and f— that.' I just said, 'Fuck off yourself,' and hung up the phone. The next day, the news editor said, 'Cliff, did you tell Mrs So and So to fuck off?' I said, 'No, but I did tell the woman that told me to fuck off quite a few times, and a few other things as well, to do exactly that. She wouldn't give me her name. Now perhaps you could go and ring up Mrs So and So and ask her if she was that woman.' Nothing more was said or heard.

We did get a little bit of praise from the public. Generally it would be a letter to the editor. People would sit down and write, rather than phone, if they enjoyed something or thought it was a good thing we did. For example, the then Prime Minister of Italy, Aldo Moro, was assassinated by the Red Brigade in a very turbulent time in the

The tape age – TV and radio

1970s. We received the syndicated coverage of the funeral service from overseas and within it was about two and a half minutes of the service (in Italian, of course) which I thought we could use in the late news. For the 7.00 pm news, we gave the story and pictures and a commentary in English, and then a pointer to tell our viewers that we would include two and a half minutes from the service in Italian in the late news. We had to quickly find an employee who could speak Italian to listen to it to make sure it was complete. Then I asked Graeme Evans, the newsreader at the time, to practice his Italian so he could let our Italian viewers know to watch the late news. He did the introduction in English and then Italian, and then went into the report. We got a bit of praise on that one – it hadn't been done before, and the powers that be were pleased too. I received a congratulatory memo. I think there must have been some good feedback from people phoning in; that generally happens. That was a highlight, one of the little triumphs I enjoyed.

One thing I never did was worry about work when I was not there. I found that very important. I was always very positive. I wouldn't let myself think about work once I had left for the day. I also remember, many times, walking out of the Tapes Room or the newsroom and being called back by one of the duty chaps who would say, 'Oh Cliff, your phone is ringing.' I would say right back, 'You go and answer it. I'm off!' Once I left the office, I never turned around to go back and pick up the phone.

When I was reporting, there was often a lot of waiting: waiting for some event, or waiting for someone to appear to give a news conference. I found I had a helpful knack of being able to sit in the back of a car and go to sleep. I would also wander around and have a look in the shop windows, and things like that. I always found something to do.

I also had a few comforting clichés and principles: for example, 'Just leave it out.' One of the things we were taught, especially when sub-editing, was when you are in doubt, leave it out. One of my principles was that you never swore if you were anywhere near a microphone. You always assumed that every microphone was alive. Now some of our politicians are still learning that, and that was one of the first things we were taught at the Vincent School of Broadcasting. Similarly, when I first started using computers, I learnt that anything you put on a computer is public knowledge no matter how many passwords you use. If you want to send something confidential, write a letter and put it in a sealed envelope.

Unwinding with your mates at the watering hole after work was also good when you need to just relax. I found riding my bicycle home afterwards was also a good way of unwinding.

I never had trouble sleeping because I never worried about work when I was not there. I found that very important. Most of the time I worked overtime, anyhow, because things would come in half an hour late. Generally I knocked off at 5.00 pm and if someone rang up at 5.30 pm – well, that was their problem! On the other hand, occasionally when the days were quiet, I had some very nice long lunches. So it all balanced out.

THE WINE AND TEA CLUBS

I had great fun at Marland House outside the Tapes Room too. I ran the tea club and the wine club. My love of wine collecting and appreciation had taken on a life of its own. In fact one of the reasons Rob and I moved out of the unit in Windsor and bought a house in East Hawthorn was to house our burgeoning wine collections. The tipping point came after we had done a four-week car trip in the Renault 12 though the wine areas of South Australia. We went to so many wineries and kept sending back a dozen bottles of this and that and various other things. We got back to Rob's parents' house to find two rather irate parents who wanted us to get rid of 28 dozen bottles of wine that were clogging up their front room, which we did.

We took the wine to my unit in Windsor and then found we had run out of space. So we set about looking for a house with a cellar.

That was a most interesting exercise; what some estate agents viewed as a cellar was clearly based more on imagination than practicality. In fact, one bloke showing us a house pulled up some floorboards in the kitchen to reveal a little square and said, 'Now, you can put a dozen bottles in there.' I replied, 'Yes, and what do I do with the other 72 dozen?' 'Oh!' At any rate, we couldn't get a house with a cellar because they cost far too much. Instead, Rob went searching and found a house in Avenue Victoria, East Hawthorn, where we eventually rebuilt the back section to create our own wine room.

It's a lovely hobby. The last time we moved, we put some 72 dozen bottles in storage until we eventually drank them out. This took five or six years and we also managed to demolish the 600 bottles of vintage port in Rob's own collection during this time.

While at the ABC, I used to get newsletters from the various vineyards which only sold wine by the dozen in those days. I didn't want to buy a whole dozen bottles of anything so I started a wine club. I used to distribute the newsletter to a whole lot of people, so they could buy a bottle or two and I'd be able to put a dozen bottles together. It meant that I could get a nice variety of wines. It was rather fun distributing the six or seven dozen bottles of wine which would arrive at the ABC newsroom from time to time. Often the news editor was involved which was just as well. Rob and I used to come back with the car at night when there was no one there to collect our not insignificant share.

I also ran a tea club during these years. I decided I would like a nice cup of brewed tea at 3.00 pm every day. I found a large electric urn and a very big 2- or 3-litre teapot and invited everyone in the newsroom to come along and have a cup of tea and a biscuit. I think I charged five or ten cents a cup to cover the costs. I would make a brew, and no matter how flat out we were at 3.00 pm, I would just yell out, 'Okay, tea is on!' And four or five people from the newsroom would put their money in and have a biscuit and a cup of tea. It was very enjoyable.

The good life

Rob found our new home in East Hawthorn. We called it Lothlorien after the happy elves in *The Lord of the Rings,* and our friends fondly called us the Lords of Lothlorien! I won't say it was a derelict house, but I can say that East Hawthorn wasn't the flavour of the month at the time, so it didn't cost too much. We spent a bit of money on it, rebuilt the back area, and turned it into very comfortable quarters, and then got two cats to run the place. Our dear old feral cat Seefah (as in 'C' for cat) from Windsor eventually succumbed to old age, and that's when we found George and Millie, two little kittens only six weeks old. I would have preferred a dog. I was a dog person in the country, and love the places they can run, but a dog was impractical in the city. As the happy Lords of Lothlorien, we celebrated George and Millie's birthday in December every year with a barbecue for our friends which became known as the 'Cats' Birthday Barbecue'. It was always well attended.

Lothlorien at 5 Avenue Victoria, East Hawthorn, October 1979

The last 'Cats' Birthday Barbecue' at Lothlorien, December 2002

We entertained at home a lot. We had a very big backyard, so big I thought I would grow my own vegetables. The only trouble was that, when I started digging, I discovered that the soil was the type of clay that the famous Hawthorn bricks are made from. Anyhow, I was lucky that I was able to dig it up using a pick and some of the farming implements I inherited from my father. Also, I was able to have a good stock of chook manure and sheep manure from my parents' farm, which was run by my cousins by then.

Working in the garden, July 1983

They didn't mind me coming out and getting the stuff. I had a couple of compost bins set up at the back, too, which I gradually built up with leaves and leftovers from cooking and all that type of thing. I was able to break the soil down and make about three beds of vegetables. I grew rhubarb, potatoes, peas, strawberries, and carrots to name a few. We did all of our own cooking; we didn't go out much in those days. I wouldn't say I was a good cook but I was a competent one. We did pretty well with our own seasonal vegetables, and we shopped at the Gleadell Street market in Richmond.

MORE TRAVEL

I wasn't home all that often as I continued to travel as much as I could with whomever I could. Mostly it was Rob but he didn't have as many holidays as me and didn't like cycling, although he did have a motorcycle at one stage, so I often had to leave him at home. I have kept a detailed log of all the trips I have made since 1936, recording where I went by date, the main places I visited, how I travelled and who I went with. Between 1972 and 1993 I managed to fit in over fifty car trips, mostly with Rob but several with other friends and even a couple with Mum and her friend, Chris Jefferies, who joined us on one occasion. I also took the odd bus trip with the Cheese Club.

Rob on his motorcycle at Lothlorien, July 1983

I had two big trips in 1987 when I took long-service leave. I began with a major solo adventure comprising a three-week car trip around

Australia, travelling 17 000 kilometres in the Toyota. At one stage I even managed a flight in a helicopter.

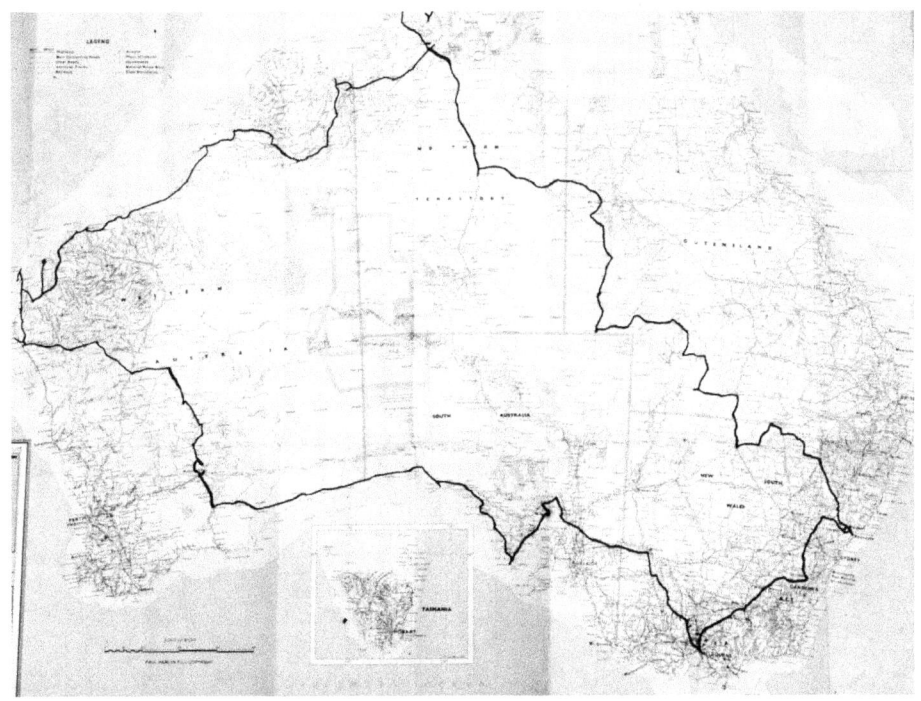

Cliff's map of his trip around Australia, August 1987

Next I travelled alone through Asia, Hong Kong China, then the Soviet Union and Scandinavia before meeting up with Rob and my sister in Reading, England. We came home via Athens and Singapore. It was marvellous to be able to show Rob so many of the best places I had been to before.

I clocked up thirteen bike trips with friends such as Colin Betts, John Crawford, Steve Kerr and Graeme Parker.

I also travelled to various parts of Australia by plane five times, including one trip to King Island with Rob and Andrew Rutherford, and did four overseas trips. In 1976, I took Rob on his first overseas

The Toyota on the Boulia–Birdsville Road in 'gibber stone' country, July 1987

In the Bell helicopter for a flight over the Katherine Gorge, July 1987

The tape age – TV and radio

At the Victoria–New South Wales border on a ride to Sydney, November 1981

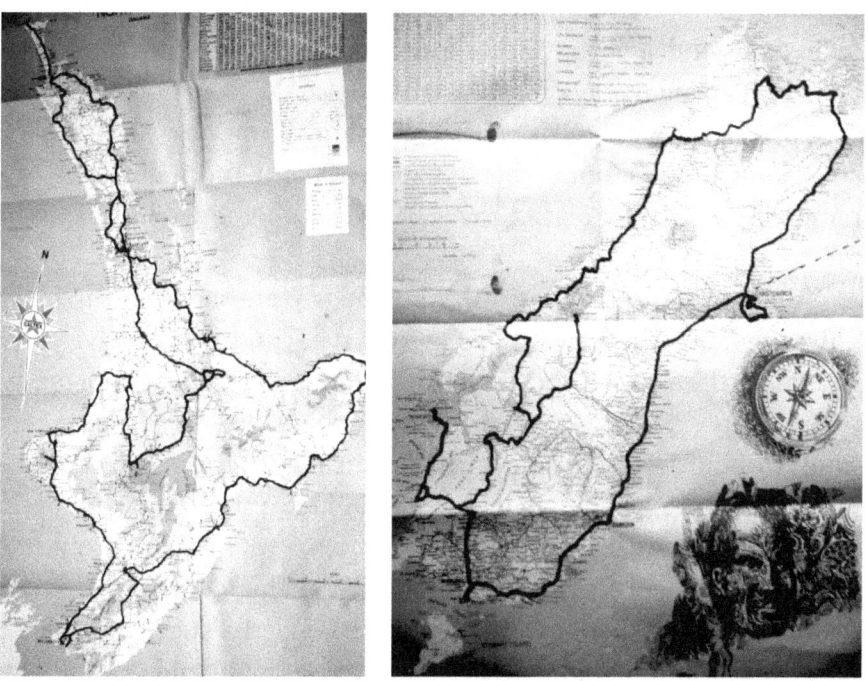

Cliff's maps of the tour of the North and South Islands of New Zealand, January 1977

trip. We went to Singapore, Malaysia and Indonesia, travelling by public transport wherever we could. Rob loved it and has been nearly as enthusiastic about travel as me ever since. The next year, in 1977 we drove around almost all of New Zealand. I went to the Philippines, Japan and Hong Kong alone in 1983, and met up with Rob in England, as mentioned above, on my long-service leave tour in 1987, and we went together to Hong Kong and Thailand in 1993.

Notching up 25 years in broadcasting

Rob often says I only worked to travel but I really did enjoy all my posts in commercial radio, commercial TV and the ABC radio and TV. I was reminded in 1984 just how far I had travelled at work since I started at 2QN Deniliquin in 1959, and what fun it had all been, when I was thrown a surprise party at a restaurant in East Hawthorn to celebrate my twenty-five years in broadcasting. Rob had collected some photos and the ABC newsroom staff had put together the most wonderful framed poster displaying photos from all parts of my broadcasting life. I have it hanging on my office wall and it is on the front cover.

Rob had also invited a great collection of my past and present colleagues. I can't remember too much about the night but I do remember that they played the ABC News theme when I came in the door.

Not long after that milestone, I notched up another – my first and only long-service leave entitlement from the ABC for my twelve years straight in the Tapes Room. It was wonderful to have an opportunity to enjoy an extended travel itinerary without having to resign this time! In hindsight, it also provided a turning point in my career. I loved the Tapes Room and in fact, I could have stayed much longer. Things were running pretty well and, about a year after my return, I indicated that I might be ready for a change. This was soon achieved when the powers that be decided that we needed a 'succession plan'; we needed to find someone or some people who could eventually take over from me.

Chapter Nine

THE COMPUTER AGE

In the late 1980s, I went back to working as Chief of Staff in radio for nearly a year. It turned out to be my last stint in the newsroom and the last days of that era of news production. A massive turning point had arrived in the industry. The old tapes were being faded out and magnificent new digital sound systems and computers were coming in. Typewriters were going and everyone was going to sit in front of their terminals and write their news directly onto computers! The ways news was being gathered, edited and broadcast were being revolutionised.

THE BASYS COMPUTER SYSTEM

The ABC chose the BASYS computer system, developed in the United States, to usher in this new age of electronic communications and computers. The BASYS system was designed to replace typewriters and telex machines with electronic-mail and copy distribution, on-screen sub-editing, teleprompting and real time updating of news items. Everyone would have access to the same raw news feeds and reporters could submit their stories instantly; instead of typing out the story on a typewriter, you could type it on the computer and it could then be transferred around from a reporter's desk to the sub-editor's desk without having to hand over a piece of paper. The pace of change was also being accelerated by the introduction of D-Cart, the digital audio system replacing analogue tapes.

As journalists and news producers, we were told that BASYS was one of the biggest computerised news systems in the world, and it would make our jobs easier, we could gather the news faster, we could work to later deadlines, and have access to a larger base of news information. However, journalists and many news room staff, particularly the News Operations Assistants (NOAs), feared their numbers would also be reduced by the introduction of BASYS; and they weren't wrong. Those journalists who remained, it was believed, would have to take on new duties of copy-taking and copy-typing into the computer. So the two unions, the ABC Staff Union and the Australian Journalists' Association (AJA), were involved in extensive negotiations.

Learning and teaching the new technology

BASYS was first introduced in 1989, and it was expected to take months of training to teach journalists and newsreaders how to use the new system. In those days, very few people knew anything about computers and most people were actually really scared of them. Initially, the ABC tried to get a couple of IT experts to teach us, the journalists, and it was hopeless. One of the things I have found in my experience with IT people is that they cannot communicate. They have not the faintest idea of how to get their message across to people who don't already know the technology. Eventually, the powers that be looked around and, as an old journalist, I was asked by one of the senior people to learn the BASYS computer system so I could train all the other journalists around Australia, and I did. The system was installed in the various newsrooms gradually over four or five years because it involved a lot of money and time and effort.

I did about four or five weeks' training on how to use a computer. Initially I learned from an IT expert, which was a bit difficult, but we got there. I also had training books and guidelines to follow, and it was a fairly simple system compared to the ones we have now. Then I went around Australia teaching the journalists how to use the system. I was the main trainer and it took four years to get around to everyone. We started off in Sydney, because the head office had to have it first, then Melbourne, Adelaide, Perth, Darwin and Tasmania. We also installed the system in the regional areas in each state so I spent time in Port Lincoln and Port Augusta in South Australia and several areas including Bunbury in Western Australia. I went everywhere – it was my dream job, really. I loved teaching and I loved travel. Only the itinerary was far from ideal. I don't know whether the chaps who were organizing the training schedule had a perverted sense of humour or just didn't quite know anything about climate, because I ended up in Canberra in freezing June, Hobart in July, where it actually snowed, Darwin in November, the suicide season, and various other places at their least favourable time! But it was still fun.

Teaching the fearful

I set up training rooms and gave each person their own computer. I made it as basic as possible. I showed them how to start up a computer: 'Press that one!' But it wasn't simple to everyone and some people were actually terrified. They were most fearful of making a mistake. The IT people had put the fear of God into them. They had been told if they made one mistake they would lose all the files or everything would collapse in a puff of smoke or something like that.

So I would sit up the front to explain and demonstrate everything from scratch: 'This is a keyboard ... when you hit this key you will see a screen a bit like a typewriter processor.' I emphasised and regularly repeated, 'If you make a mistake don't panic! I will show you how to fix or delete it.' I also used to play 'chopsticks' on the keyboard or just hit the keys at random to get them familiar with the whole setup.

My teaching method was straightforward. If I had a group of about five, six or seven people, I would have them seated in a semi-circle in front of me. I would have a whiteboard at the front of the room, I'd go through what we were going to do, and they would listen and then we would all do it. I would then stand behind each of them and watch their screens to see who had mastered the idea and who was getting lost. Later, I would explain the concepts of directories and files. As the group became more familiar with the computers we learnt more complex functions.

I used to make sure that, after about an hour and half, there was a break of half an hour where people could absorb the information, ask any questions and have a cup of coffee. And then we'd go on to the next step and so on. By the end of the day when they were getting mentally tired – it is tiring learning something new – we might just spend the last half an hour revising what we had gone through and how far we got. So that was my method of teaching, and it worked very well.

It was a great program. I really enjoyed it and only stopped because I had run out of people to train. I was happy to continue to travel around the country and train people in the regional stations, as I had done in Bunbury, Port Lincoln, Port Augusta and Burnie and across Victoria, of course. But the ABC decided that it was much cheaper, in future, to get someone who had been trained in a capital city to train their own regional staff.

THE ULTIMO TRANSITION PROJECT

I wasn't without a new mission for long, however, because it was around this time that the new Sydney studios in Ultimo were being built, and I was transferred to work on the Ultimo Transition Team. This was an horrendous project and I had a difficult time.

The building for the new state-of-the-art headquarters was going up on schedule but no-one in the Sydney branch was in a hurry to leave their comfortable little empires in King's Cross. The Forbes Street studios had been sold to a developer who had extended the lease for a few years. All of a sudden, he decided that he was going to clear the place out one day and pull the building down the next. It was then discovered that nothing was being done locally and there were various excuses. David Hill, the then General Manager, went berserk when he found out how badly the move was being organised. He quickly set up the Ultimo Transition Team to manage the move. The team was headed by a Queenslander and comprised 30 people who were taken from every state except New South Wales. The team flew to Sydney each week and back to their respective homes on the weekend, paid for by the New South Wales branch because they had mismanaged things so badly.

ABC Building, Harris Street, Ultimo with office tower added in 2002

The worst thing for me was when I was mugged in Kings Cross after a few drinks after work one night. I was hit on the head with a brick and was badly injured. I had my wallet and my father's watch stolen. I spent a few days in hospital and was still a dreadful sight, according to Rob, when he picked me up at the airport in Melbourne.

The team was responsible for training the technicians and journalists to use the equipment in the new studios. I was there to teach people how to use the BASYS system and also, because the ABC was going into computerised digital work at that time, I was learning a bit about that too. It was very hectic time for me, flying to Sydney every Monday morning, staying with a friend during the week and flying back every Friday night. I did that for three months. I might add that it did put a lot of 'bikkies in the barrel'.

At the end of the Transition Project, I went back to my contact at the ABC and said, 'Okay I'll go keep going round training people'.

But they said, 'No, we haven't got enough money for that'. I know where it was all spent! I said, 'Okay', and that's when I went to see my accountant and put two and two together. It seemed as though, at 57, I could retire. After working your whole life, when you're told you don't really have to work anymore, it sounds like a good idea! So I retired.

Retirement, briefly

After thirty wonderful years in radio and television in both national and commercial broadcasting, I left the ABC on 30 July 1993. I wrote to the news editor at the time to inform her of my departure. I advised that I would miss the excitement of the big stories but I wouldn't be missing the tyranny of rosters. I added that I would be happy to continue to consult for ABC if they had any issues with the BASYS training though. I had very mixed feelings, both celebration and sadness, but I was leaving on a high.

The Head of News and Current Affairs accepted my resignation and congratulated me on my dedication and commitment. In particular, he mentioned my work with BASYS. He said, 'Not everybody, towards the end of such a long career, would have been inclined, or able, to take on new technology and become a recognised expert. It is to your credit, and to the ABC's benefit, that you've done so.'

I felt lucky to have been in such a fast-moving industry during a time of such enormous change. To be there as the news was transformed, and to contribute to that transformation in my own way, was a true honour and a privilege.

Back to BASYS

I did retire, and was ready to go for a drive around Australia, but not for long. Within a week, the manager of the BASYS company, whom I knew quite well, rang me up and said, 'I suppose you are making a nuisance of yourself and have nothing to do?' I said, 'Yeah.' He went on, 'My full-time trainer has retired.' I quickly pointed out that I didn't want a full-time job. He said, 'No, I know you don't. I don't want a full-time trainer. I want a part-time trainer who can do jobs on a consulting basis.' He told me about the consulting fee and the living away allowance, and that he just wanted me to do occasional jobs in Australia and overseas. 'Are you interested?' he asked. 'Oh, yes!' I said. 'Good, next week I've booked you on a plane to Hong Kong to start at one of the television stations there,' he announced.

So I headed off to do some work at a commercial radio and television station in Hong Kong. Soon after I went back for a second round in Hong Kong and added another station in Kuala Lumpur in Malaysia to the list, and was able to take Rob with me. It was great again to combine my love of travel with work, and overseas this time. There were also some new challenges teaching the staff in Hong Kong to keep me interested.

Mobile phones had arrived but not many people had them at the time. Some of the hierarchy did and one man in Hong Kong carried his along to class and, of course, his phone rang in the middle of the class. I thought, 'Hum. I don't like this.' But I said, 'Oh, will the class please be silent? I am sure this is a very important phone call for Mr So and So.' By this time, he was cringing. 'We will wait for you to finish your call – it is important, obviously. You wouldn't have interrupted the class otherwise,' I continued. I never had any trouble with mobile phones after that.

I loved teaching and getting the message across but it wasn't always easy. One of the problems was that there were a lot of non-journalists in the class who didn't need to be there. Because they feared losing face, they wouldn't ask questions, which compromised their learning. For others, their English language skills just weren't good enough. English might have been their third language; they might speak the local Chinese dialect, and Cantonese or Mandarin, and then English thrown in. The journalists were quite good with English, so there was no problem there. As I pointed out to them all,

I couldn't speak any Chinese so they had to put up with it. I had had to learn a few other languages over the years but I didn't really have time to learn Mandarin. Also, too, you have to be very careful with Chinese because it is more about tone. If you get the tone wrong, you can say very insulting things without realising it.

In addition, I found out that there were a lot of language problems with English when people were trained by Americans. I remember I was talking about, 'Don't forget to put the full stop in.' One particular man looked bewildered, and no-one was doing as I had asked. All of a sudden I asked, 'Who taught you English?' 'An American.' I said, 'Right. Put the period in.' 'Ah.' Little things like that.

I really enjoyed teaching journalists how to use computers, and helping them take up the fantastic new broadcasting opportunities presented by the digital age. I did it for three years, and would have happily continued on a part-time and occasional basis. Inevitably, we ran out of customers once the BASYS system was fully implemented across all the newsrooms and the stations were able to train their own staff and to affiliate stations independently. I retired for the second and final time after my last mission in Brisbane in 1996.

Chapter Ten

RETIREMENT AND EVEN MORE FUN!

Having already travelled the world, and with a long-established host of hobbies and social activities, retirement simply meant more time to do all my favourite things and enjoy some wonderful new pursuits. I was very relaxed about the prospect of life without work. I looked forward to spending more time on philately, long lunches, and staying at home playing our CDs, reading newspapers and doing the crosswords. In fact, when people asked me how I felt about retiring, I could honestly say that I thought about it only once, for no more than a millisecond, and certainly never regretted the freedom of my new retiree status. It was a seamless transition for me.

Once I left, I found I could do all these things and more, such as volunteer work for the Flying Doctor Service, the Olympic and Commonwealth Games, the football club and a host of other things. In the travel department, I also found plenty of day trips to keep me amused and later there were bigger travel plans.

NEW FAVOURITES

One of the first things I did was join the ABC Reunion Club. This group of ex-ABC staffers met monthly for lunch and a range of other activities including day trips and overnight coach trips around Victoria. This suited my fondness for long lunches and regional travel very well! I did about eight trips with them over the next five years. I also served on the Committee, as did Rob who was Treasurer for sixteen years. I was also President for four years before handing over to a younger group of ex-ABC people.

For similar reasons I didn't need much persuasion to join the 'Red Brigade'. Friends told me about it: 'Oh, you've got to come along, as you're not doing anything.' So I did. It began, and remained, as a group of people who enjoyed good red wine, good company and good restaurants that could be reached by public transport, preferably trains. It was initially called the 'Red Brigade' because we drank copious amounts of red wine, and secondly as a reference to the Italian Red Brigade as we liked to think we were 'restaurant terrorists'!

While membership was open to anyone, most people were ex-school teachers or ex-ABC or they had friends who were with the ABC, and it just grew. There's no formal structure. We haven't got a chairman. We haven't got a secretary, or a fixed schedule. We just sort of work together and it's a bit of fun.

The Red Brigade at Amici Trattoria, Camberwell, November 2015. Left to right, Gary Kennedy, Carol Wilson, Peter Watling, Cliff Peel, Gerry McKechnie, Rob Young, Graeme Wilson, Peggy Tipping, Doug Tipping, Neil Hobbs, Linton Bryant, Graham Fettling, Alan Solomon.

It started with someone in the group saying, 'I know a nice restaurant in Ballarat', or maybe Bendigo was suggested. They went there to lunch and found that they rather enjoyed it. Next, someone suggested a restaurant in Geelong that they had enjoyed, and so the idea just grew. So everyone would know when and where we were going, we decided to go on the third Wednesday of every month. We take the train, along with some bottles of red wine, to a nice restaurant for lunch. It's a bit of travel by train as well, which I enjoy. Any member can organise a trip. There are between ten and twelve members, maybe up to twenty of us in a big one. Now we call that little ensemble the Country Diners from Melbourne – the CDFM group.

We've been to places like Geelong, Drouin, Woodend and Ballarat. There we call in at Craig's Hotel and have a glass of sparkling wine to sort of set us on the journey. Most recently we went back to Ballarat, and next time it will be Castlemaine. We get to see some of the best restaurants from all around, but we have a few requirements. The restaurants have to be BYO, and we've got to be able to get there by train; we don't drive. They have to be within walking distance of the station. Shepparton is the furthest we go. The restaurant there is about twenty-five minutes' walk from the station, but still within reach. We use our seniors' cards together with the off-peak day returns, which makes the travel very cheap. It costs only a quarter of the normal price for travel on a weekday. We go there on the morning train which is off-peak, returning in the middle of the afternoon which is also off-peak to Melbourne people. If the restaurant is a bit far away from the station we might think of taking a taxi or local bus, but generally we can walk back to the station. The walk back is already easier because we've all had our fill. By the time we get back on the train, we are ready for a bit of a doze.

Over the years we have found some really lovely little restaurants. I know at Shepparton they are very happy to see us too, because they advertise that they're so good that they attract diners from Melbourne for lunch. We don't mind that.

Volunteer work

The flying doctor service

Perhaps inspired by my namesake, John Clifford Peel, I worked for the Flying Doctor Service for many years from 1992 to 2000. I used to help them regularly with various fund-raising campaigns. This usually meant putting letters asking for donations into envelopes, licking the envelopes and posting them – basically helping with the mail-outs. We sent out hundreds and thousands of letters. Once we also hand-wrote the addresses, working on a clever ploy that while people might throw away a mass-produced letter from a charity, they would be more likely to open a hand-written envelope with a stamp on it. That strategy did work. I left when the Board changed direction and involved fewer volunteers in their mail-out campaigns and their headquarters moved from St Kilda Road to Richmond.

Cliff wearing the Sydney Olympic Games volunteers' uniform, September 2000

The Sydney Olympic and Paralympic Games

In the 2000 Olympic Games I volunteered to work in the press rooms or the press corps. Basically, it was a media support role. I was helping journalists from around the world to find out what they needed to know. I helped answer their questions, gave them directions to news conferences and made sure that they had the facilities that they wanted.

I then stayed on and did the same thing for the Paralympic Games which followed. That was much more fun because I was working in the main stadium. I had a team of teenagers from one of the schools working as my helpers. Basically the job was again supporting journalists, distributing results and helping them to find the information they needed. I received recognition certificates and I've still got the uniforms.

The Melbourne Commonwealth Games

I performed much the same role at the Commonwealth Games in Melbourne in 2006. I worked as a retired old journalist does when dealing with current journalists. The journalists can't push you around because you have 'been there and done that'. I remember once at the Olympic Games one of the chaps came barging in and said, 'I am from the *New York Times*. I want this that and the other thing quickly. I am running late for a news conference.' I turned around and said, 'I have been a journalist for thirty years. I have yet to find a journalist who has been on time. Now wait your turn!' There were no problems after that.

Prahran Football Club

I have always followed Prahran Football club and the VFA (Victorian Football Association). I first offered to help in 1989 when I started my teaching role and had my weekends off. I went down to the club and offered my help. Prahran wasn't the richest club at the time, and so they said, 'Oh, yes. But we can't pay you.' I said, 'Oh, that's all right.' I did some time-keeping there and ended up as the last team manager before the club was unable to field a team in 1993.

Meanwhile, Southbank Amateur Football Club had been formed from the amateur players of the former State and Commonwealth Bank teams, which had been disbanded when the banks were privatised in the early 1990s. They were joined in 1994 by a lot of the former Prahran players who just wanted to play football whether they were paid or not. A couple of the administrators and I got phone calls saying, 'You had better come and do something useful.'

I went across to Southbank and was there for quite some time as a time-keeper and ended up being a goal umpire. By 1999, Prahran Football Club got its act together again financially and the two clubs formally merged. We changed our name back to the Prahran Amateur Football Club and then later again to the Prahran/Assumption Football Club when the old boys from Assumption College in Kilmore joined us. We also returned to our oval at Toorak Park after Southbank was forced out of their home oval, which is now the multi-purpose stadium at Melbourne Park.

Over the years, I've pretty much done every odd job imaginable there, except be on the committee which I avoided like the plague. I don't like football committees; too time-consuming and too much politics. I was the team manager, goal umpire, time-keeper, and worked on the score board and even in the bar. In amateur associations, everyone has to do everything. If someone was ill or hadn't turned up, I would hear, 'Cliff, go over and work the score board.' So you could say I was basically an all-rounder. I'd just help out where I could, whatever job came up. I mainly did goal umpiring and kept doing that until I was about 70. Then I decided that I didn't want to be the oldest goal umpire in the association, so I took up time-keeping.

Rob and I are both still members, so whenever we're not going out anywhere on a Saturday, we go to watch Prahran/Assumption play at Toorak Park. I was made a Life Member in 2001. I was pretty chuffed about that.

STAMP COLLECTING

Over the years, I've become a serious philatelist which is just a fancy name for a stamp collector. I got the interest from my mother who was a keen collector; her collection went back to the 1920s. Right from when I was very young, Mum used to bring out her album for us to look at together. She used to tell me where each stamp came from and I loved little coloured pictures. Mum had a missionary friend who sent back interesting stamps from the New Hebrides (now Vanuatu) and later from China. Eventually I inherited Mum's stamp collection.

I got my first stamp album and started my own collection when I was about five or six. I was always interested in the story behind every stamp. I loved the older stamps, and the ones from the 1940s and 1950s in particular. At that stage, there wasn't the prolific range of stamps that we get now as post offices churn them out each month just to raise revenue. In those days, new stamps were still issued fairly regularly but there was generally a good reason or a good story behind the new release.

The history recorded in stamps is also quite interesting. I can name practically all of the Kings of Yugoslavia from the time the Prince of Serbia became King of Yugoslavia, Serbia and Croatia, and the various ones assassinated in the ensuing twenty years before the Communists threw them out. Of course, a lot of the earlier stamps featured the royal families of particular countries which now no longer exist. Many provinces have issued stamps only briefly. For example, there were six states in Australia that all issued stamps before federation: Victoria, New South Wales, Queensland, Tasmania, Western Australia, and South Australia.

I have now a grand total of sixty-seven stamp albums. People ask me how I have collected so many! I explain that it has happened over time. I started very young and was an avid collector during my school days. When I left school and went into broadcasting, I was travelling too frequently to take my albums with me. I didn't have as many then so I left them at my parents' place until I settled down and got my own unit. Really, I was always collecting stamps to a certain extent but not in enormous quantities.

Then I had the opportunity to get a bit more serious. One of my friends said if I was interested I could have his album because he'd given it all up. I took that album and then, when we bought the house in East Hawthorn I had more room, and that's when I started really getting more serious about stamps.

I bought Neil Munro's albums and an album from a friend in Sydney who didn't want to continue his collection. Another friend, whose father left him the collection, wasn't interested at all so we had it valued and I bought it from him. That gave me three lots. By this time I was retired and had a bit more time on my hands at home. Then I went down to the Charles Leski Auctions and bought what they call a 'suitcase', which is a collection of stamps that collectors have thrown together or have never sorted out for the past thirty years – a complete mess. I bought a suitcase for only about $600. I started sorting that out and then I thought, 'I've got all these stamps in my own collection. I've really got to get them in order'. That's when I started the present form of albums that I've got now.

I sorted them all out and put them into the sixty-seven albums that I keep here. It took me a couple of years. I did it country by country and put all the stamps in chronological order, leaving spaces for those missing, and when I finished each country I typed out a sheet listing every stamp that was missing. Stamps come in sets. Sometimes it's just a single stamp, other times there's a whole range of values and different designs on the set issued to mark a particular anniversary, or another reason for putting out the stamp, like a 50th anniversary of this or that.

Fortunately, I completed a full review of my collection before I had my recent eye problem with macular degeneration. I looked at every stamp. It took me about three or four months, just taking it bit by bit. It allowed me to ensure my list was correct, and I did find a few errors. It also gave me the chance to see my collection, the whole lot. I was really pleased about that because now I would have difficulty. Occasionally, I can look something up, using a magnifying glass, to remind myself about certain stamps or details, but fortunately I have a pretty good idea of what is in there.

I have my favourite stamps, of course, and a number of those are over 100 years old. For example, I have a Penny Black, the first stamp issued in the UK in 1840. I also have every Australian stamp issued, which is called a 'simple collection' of each issue. It includes every stamp issued but not all the variations of each stamp. The value is not about how old a stamp is but how few there are. I have one stamp that's probably worth $5000.

I stopped collecting stamps after the end of the second millennium, 31 December 2000, because they were being issued too often and I couldn't keep up. Now my only intention is just to fill up all the gaps in these albums; the list itself takes up four binders. I have documented the stamps I have and those I don't using the Stanley Gibbons' catalogue number system, which allocates a number to every stamp. This is the bible for stamp collectors. It means I can say to a dealer, 'I want the various stamp 647', and they will know exactly which stamp I need. I figure it should take me about three lifetimes and a couple of million dollars to complete my collection. But while I've got the chance, I'll continue doing it.

I have also had the opportunity to sort out a number of neglected collections through my stamp collecting for the Red Cross. When people know I collect for the Red Cross they often ask me to review their old collections. I tell them what I think and a couple of times I offer to put it into a stock book which will be in alphabetical order by country and chronological order by stamps. My cost is that any stamp I want for my collection, I can have. A couple of people agreed to this. I got a few stamps and it was fun. Otherwise, once a year I take in a box of stamps that I have separated from their envelopes and donate them to the Red Cross. They in turn sell them at their stalls and also sell them to dealers who may in turn sell them overseas where there is a larger market. They still won't pay more than the face value of them. Even the new, unused or unmarked stamps still sell below their face value.

I've really enjoyed stamp collecting over my lifetime because it's taught me so much about the history of places, and the geography. When I went travelling and saw something like the White Tower at Thessaloniki in Greece, I would say, 'Oh, I've got that on a stamp.' Then I'd try to take a photo of it from the same angle that was on the stamp. It's a bit of fun. Sending postcards back home was an essential part of my travels. We could track how many days I'd been in each place based on the number of postcards my mother, and later Rob, got from each country.

The collection, all sixty-seven albums of stamps, is worth quite a lot, but I couldn't say how much. But it's not a monetary thing – it's not there as a financial investment. I have just enjoyed collecting them and had the real thrill, so many times, of seeing a place that I'd originally seen on a stamp. I love being reminded of the places I've been when I flick through the stamp albums. I could have them insured, but they would end up being locked away and I'd never have a chance to look through them. I certainly couldn't replace it. My philosophy is that it's something I've collected over seventy-five years and you can't replace your history. Some things you just have to enjoy for what they are; there's nothing to be gained from trying to hang onto everything forever.

A POSTCARD A DAY ...

I've always loved sending postcards home, one per day when away, and always with a local stamp from wherever I was at the time. I started this habit on my first big trip in 1968 by sending Mum a postcard every day to share my travels and let her know that I was still alive. I couldn't afford to phone home in those days, and certainly not every day.

I did the same for Rob when he was left at home. He would have a copy of my itinerary, and he knew exactly where I was each day. We didn't have mobile phones until recently so I would drop him a postcard so he could track where I was. Rob has developed a great collection of postcards as a result. They tie in really well with the stamps. He didn't usually worry too much about me, because he knew where I was and what I was seeing. Where possible, Rob has travelled with me. Being apart isn't always ideal, but absence does make the heart grow fonder.

Photography and my slide collection

I have had a camera all my life. I started with a box Brownie which I used throughout my school days. It was a great camera. I moved on to a SLR camera on my eighteenth birthday which I took on all my travels. I gave Rob a camera early on in our life together. He took to it instantly and is now the cameraman.

While I do have a very good memory, and can generally take myself back to anywhere I have been, if I am not too sure, I can look up my slide catalogue to see where I was on a particular day and then see the photos to prove it! I have over 10 000 slides, all listed by date, subject and place. I have coded them from A1 01 to LZ36. So I can either look up the date or the place in my slide catalogues and find the actual slide by its code within two minutes. For example, on 29 July 1972, I was on the lookout at Whitfield, near Wangaratta. To look at the picture, which is number CH30, I find the CHs on the side of the box and go to slide 30. I can find it in no time at all. To view the picture, we use a little portable viewer, or we can set up the full slide projector to see them on a wall or a screen.

Move to Prospect Hill Road

After twenty-six years at Lothlorien in Hawthorn, and having happily paid off the mortgage, the fences needed replacing again. We had built new fences when we first arrived because the place was pretty dilapidated. We had the most dilapidated price too, which was good, but I didn't want to go through it again. By that time I was getting on too; I was 67. So I said to Rob, 'No. I'm not going to go put up those fences again. I think we're going to sell the place. We're going to downsize.' Later, as I walked along Prospect Hill Road, Camberwell, I saw a sign announcing that retirement units were being built there. To me, it also said, 'Position, position, position!' I made some inquiries and talked Rob into having a look.

We went along to see the salesman, David Macrae, and saw a model of the retirement village and the plans. We liked it, chose the unit we wanted, and Rob and I pulled out $50 each on the spot as a holding deposit. We were one of the first residents to move in. Technically, Rob was too young to be a resident. He was 53 when we signed up so we had had to get a special dispensation on the contract to cover the gap until he turned 55. Twelve years later, Rob is still the youngest resident at Prospect Hill Village.

Prospect Hill Village, Camberwell, September 2004

It was the second time I had bought 'off the plan'. Irving Avenue, where Rob and I really started our lives together, was a great success and Prospect Hill Village is where we expect to remain for the duration.

As with Irving Avenue, and practically every organisation I have belonged to – Prahran Football Club excepted – I soon joined the Residents' Committee and served as Secretary for a number of years and Chairman for one term. These were pleasant jobs. Occasionally a resident has a concern, but it really does run very well because we have an excellent management company. I also volunteered to help run the bar on a rostered basis every Friday afternoon for Happy Hour. We also join in many of the other activities and trips. We feel we really belong here. As a gay couple, and in fact the only gays in the village we think, the community has always been very welcoming and accepting which we have appreciated.

Life with Rob, at home and away

Rob and I have had a very long and successful partnership which we both continue to appreciate. It's now forty-four years since we first met! We connected then and, despite the age difference (I was 35 and Rob was only 22), it has worked ever since. Apart from our separate pursuits, my love of stamps and bike riding, and Rob's love of cross-stitch and his clock collection, we share mostly all the same interests. We are opposites when it comes to religion – I am a devoted atheist and Rob is a practising Catholic, and quite active in the local Our Lady of Victories parish in Burke Road, Camberwell. We both love travel, particularly rail travel, photography, the long-lunch groups, red wine, football and music – we have a fabulous range of CDs from classical opera to classic pop and country music.

When we are asked about the secret of a successful relationship, we both agree on three main things: tolerance, love and support. Of course, like any couple we have had our moments, and we are opposites in temperament, but Rob has always given me support and love when I've needed it. He has always been there to come home to, especially during the hard times when I was working long hours or commuting from Sydney. On the few occasions he wasn't there, because he was working or something else, he was always there in spirit. I knew he would turn up sometime and I could talk to him, tell him my woes and he would listen and support me. Sharing things with Rob has been one of the most important things for me.

Rob's rock

Rob, who is far more extravagant with language than me, says,

> Cliff is my saviour, my rock and mentor, and anybody who could stay living with me should be awarded an OBE with KCMG bars! Cliff's greatest virtue is his tolerance and patience, and he plays a lot of Patience, the card game, too. I don't know where I would be, or which bridge I would be under, without Cliff. He helps me calm down when I get a bit stressed or can't find things. He is a frustrated clerk. Everything he has done is written down in columns that balance down and balance across. He does his books every day. He has his finger on the pulse. He knows exactly at any point in time how much money is in his wallet. He has an extremely annoying habit of leaving drawers open, ajar, not closing cupboards – I shan't go on. It's been a privilege to be associated with Cliff and I am one of the luckiest boys around.

Fortunately, Rob's parents liked me. We used to have dinner at their place and Rob's mum was over the moon after I came back for seconds of fricasseed rabbit – she did a beautiful rabbit. She is oft-quoted as saying, 'Thank God for Cliff!' and told Rob that I was the best thing that ever happened to him! My parents also liked Rob. They never knew, or did not acknowledge, our true relationship, and I never told them. When Rob arrived and looked like he was staying, Mum just accepted him as part of the family, and Dad did too. Rob has attended all my family events ever since. My uncles and cousins were also fully accepting which was not expected in such a conservative country family. I was surprised too when we were just introduced casually as, 'Cliff and his friend Rob' on occasions such as Mum's 80th or 90th birthdays. On the other hand, when you look at them now, I think they're all pretty open-minded.

In those days, and earlier, I had to be very cautious. We couldn't be as open as we are today. To start with, homosexuality was illegal (right up until 1981 in Victoria). People were getting arrested all over the place. They were often entrapped and also blackmailed; we heard so many stories. One of our dear friends tragically committed suicide by carbon monoxide poisoning in the garage at home, because his mother didn't recognise or couldn't cope with the fact that her son was gay. He was under terrible stress. And there were others, too. There were also terrible financial penalties regarding inheritance and superannuation. Rob and I were delighted to be one of the first couples to apply for and receive a Relationship Certificate soon after the Relationship Register was established. Our certificate is number 86 and dated 15 January 2009. This has worked very well for us; so well that we have no need or wish to go through a wedding ceremony when gay marriage inevitably becomes recognised.

Cliff at his desk, 2009

Travelling together

Rob has also been a fantastic travelling companion and we have travelled together whenever it was possible. I have had to do so many trips alone, and the one thing I really missed was have someone to share experiences with and talk about them afterwards. I have really loved being able to share my favourite places with Rob and to discover new places together. Rob also loves train travel as much as me, which is remarkable. His main complaint about trains and travelling on them, he says, is that the journeys are too short. He jokes that if you could increase the time on the train, and preferably double it, such as the trip we did across India, he'd go again!

I took Rob on his first overseas trip in 1976 and we have never looked back. He also joined me on the second leg of my six months' long-service leave around the world trip in 1987 – my second biggest adventure. I did the first part solo, which mean going into areas I had never been before on my own, so it was reminiscent of my first around the world trip. The main allure for me was to travel on the famous Trans-Siberian Express which, during the Soviet Union days, was a different story than it is now. There were no luxury trains and tourist trains then. It was just an ordinary train, part of the regular Trans-Siberian rail service, with very two very basic classes.

Cliff on the Great Wall of China, September 1987

To start off, I flew to Hong Kong. I took the train from Hong Kong to Canton (now Guangzhou) in China. At that time Hong Kong was a British possession. And then I had to go into Communist China. I took the Beijing Express from Guangzhou to Beijing. I wandered around Beijing for a couple of days, and had a look at the Great Wall among other key attractions. From there I took the Trans-Mongolian Express from Beijing through Ulan Bator to Irkutsk in Siberia. Interestingly for me, at the Mongolian border they lift the train off its standard gauge bogies (train wheels) and transfer it to a broad gauge which was installed by the Czars throughout the Russian empire which then included Mongolia. You could go to a viewing platform and actually watch this happening. Cranes were used to lift the carriages up so the old bogies could be rolled out and the new ones rolled under.

It was fun complying with the various passport checks. For example, the Mongolian people were very worried about people bringing any subversive literature into the country on the train. They tended to look for books, and we were warned to keep any books we might have out of view. At the Tibet checkpoint, we got some Chinese government tourist pamphlets on visiting Shanghai and seeing the Tomb of the Terracotta Warriors and scattered these on the table in our compartment. They dutifully came in and examined it all very seriously, said, 'All right', and that was it. They had seen the acceptable literature.

We had to go through the Mongolian–Russian border crossing very late at night, around midnight, which was a bit of a pain. Four of us were in a compartment with bunks that could fold up into seats during the day. The train stopped at Ulan Bator, the capital of Mongolia, for two or three hours and I was offered a tour for about two hours while the train was there that would have cost me about $400 dollars. I thought, 'Yeah, I'll take that tour. It is very expensive but I will never see Ulan Bator again so I might as well have a look.' Then, just before I was leaving, the travel agent doubled the cost to US$950. I said, 'Not going. No go. Too steep.' It was just the fee of the greedy Communist government that was going broke. I saw Ulan Bator from the station. People who went on the trip said I didn't miss anything.

Unlike my first train trip, I was enjoying the comfort of 'soft class'. There were two different types of comfort; soft class and hard class. In soft class you have four people and we had two women and two men so you had to organise yourselves in terms of getting changed and so on. There were toilets at the end of the corridors, and there was a wash basin in our compartment. There was a samovar, a Russian vessel for boiling water, at the end of each carriage where you could make tea.

I remember in the morning on route to Irkutsk, I was having breakfast on the train in the dining car. I remember being just so delighted to see Lake Baikal below us as we came down through the mountains. Lake Baikal is the oldest and deepest freshwater lake in the world. I thought, 'This is fantastic! This is international travel! Here I am in the dining car looking at the waters of Lake Baikal.'

We boarded the famous Trans-Siberian Train – the longest train journey in the world – at Irkutsk. It took four days to get to Moscow. We left on 11 September and we got to Moscow on the evening of the 15th. It was an interesting train, and it is the only way to travel across Russia. I don't know how many run a day, but it was quite regular. I was told that we would stay for about 15 minutes at each station but then move off without any warning whistles or announcements. Fortunately, our conductor was very good: he would come to the door and yell, and herd us back in. If we missed a train, we could wait and catch another but we may or may not have seen our bags again. They would either have turned up in Moscow after us or been sold on the black market. So you made sure you didn't miss the train.

On the train itself, the dining car, as a good communist operation, was opened at local time and we went through ten time zones! It would open at 9.00 am, close at midday so the staff could have lunch, pity about the passengers ... and be closed again at 5.00 pm. So we organised breakfast at 10.00 am, knowing that for an hour at least we had a chance of getting some food, and we went for dinner at 4.00 pm for the same reason. Not that there was much to choose from. The menu was generally black bean soup and borscht, which is a sort of minced-meat soup with potatoes and maybe greens if you were lucky. You couldn't buy alcohol but they had good fruit juices made from pears and peaches and stone fruits.

You weren't supposed take your own alcohol but I did. I had my bottle of vodka. A Chinese chap on the same carriage had a bottle of Chinese brandy which he would share as long as I gave him a drink of vodka. The Chinese brandy was a real, shall we say, strong drink.

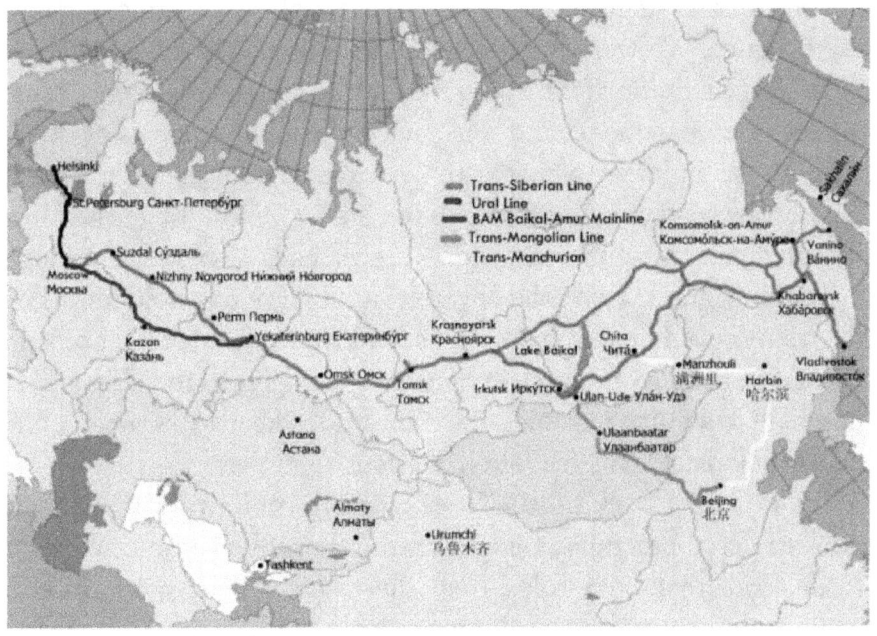

The various routes along the Trans-Siberian Line

The train finally got to Moscow and we did the usual tourist things. We visited Red Square and the Cathedral of the Assumption inside the Kremlin. I did do a tour of the Kremlin and also visited Lenin's Tomb.

Then on to St Petersburg or Leningrad, as it was then, on the normal overnight commuter train which was still quite interesting. I was particularly impressed with the rebuilding of the Summer Palace of Peter the Great after the Second World War. It had been restored beautifully, right back to its original splendour, and probably even better than it was before the German army blew it to bits.

Next I took the train to Helsinki. Crossing the Russian–Finnish border was quite an experience. This was the toughest border crossing I've ever done. Russia was paranoid about anyone leaving the Communist-dominated Union of Soviet Socialist Republics. At the border crossing there was a six-metre high fence stretching into the distance. We were in a three-carriage train. There were armed guards on each side of the train. They walked on the roof. They came into my compartment, and unscrewed the ceiling panels to see if anyone was hidden up there. They searched underneath the train for stowaways trying to get out of the Soviet Union. I had the most thorough search of my luggage I've ever had. They went through everything, and I wasn't the only one, as other people told me. Then the train moved on a short distance, and we were able to get off and we had to hand over all our rubles in exchange for Finnish markka, not that I had much in rubles. I was allowed to keep as a souvenir one five-kopek piece, worth about half a cent.

Then we got back on the three-carriage train. It took about an hour to get about thirty people on the train by the time we went through all this rigmarole. Then the train, still with its Russian engine and drivers on board, crept slowly across a hundred metres of clear land until we reached the Finnish forest. Then the driver hit the accelerator. I've never felt a diesel take off so fast, as if to say, 'We're out of here!' We stopped at a little station about 10 kilometres further into Finland, where electric overhead wires appeared, and the staff took the Russian diesel engine off and put on a Finnish electric engine. Three Finnish customs officers came on board, one to each carriage. 'Passports, please', in Russian, English, and Finnish. I showed my Australian passport and he just handed it back. 'Welcome to Finland', he said. That was it. I think they reckoned if you got through the Communist blockade you were to be congratulated.

Then I took the train from Finland north of Helsinki, up to Boden on the Swedish–Finnish border where we had to change trains and go onto the standard gauge Swedish trains, which again were very comfortable. I went as far as Narvik in Norway, which is the furthermost point of the railway line. I know when we crossed the Arctic Circle, the train slowed down and they told us that we'd see the pole which marked the Arctic Circle on the left-hand side. We could take photos, so we did. I knew we were in the Arctic Circle, but it was about fifteen or sixteen degrees that day.

The journey continued by criss-crossing the country back to Stockholm and from there to Gothenburg. I met up with a person in Gothenburg who I'd first met in Kalgoorlie, and went to his place. I missed the last train, so I had to sleep on the station until 4.00 am. (I missed the train because I had stayed too long in the bar, which has happened on the odd occasion before on my travels.)

From Gothenburg, I travelled to Oslo and on to Myrdal. From there I took a very interesting railway line down to a little place called Flam, which is on the head of a fjord. Mother went there many years ago, and said, 'You must go down there!' Now, the railway drops about a thousand metres, I think, and it does a spiral inside the mountain as it descends. The track emerges from the mountain in several places as well, and the views are marvellous.

While we were waiting at Myrdal, there was quite a delay, and one of the railway staff who spoke English asked, 'Are you going down to Flam?' When I replied that I was, he said, 'Right. Hop on the train there. That little train is taking you down.' It was about two or three carriages. He said, 'We're actually going to give you a free trip, because we've got to take some railway workers half-way down to where they live, the village there. Hop on board and we'll go down, and then we've got to bring you back because we've got to wait for another train coming from the other direction. Then we'll take you right down to Flam.' I went half-way down and it was rather fun, and came back again to Myrdal. Then we took the full trip.

By this time it was getting dark, and I was booked into the hotel near the station. This was on 1 October 1987. There were no lights on, except just one on the front door. I thought, 'This looks completely closed!' I knocked on the door and rang the bell. The door opened. 'Ah, you're Mr Peel from Australia?' I agreed that I was, and he invited me in. The hotel had closed after the summer season. It was the first weekend after the closing, but they had received my booking from Australia. The caretaker, who lived in the hotel all the time, told me all this. He had agreed to look after a visitor from Australia, so I was able to stay there even though the hotel was officially closed for winter. I had a beautiful smorgasbord for dinner. I enjoyed that and then was given the best room in the hotel; no-one else was there.

Then came the highlight of the whole trip. As the sun rose in the morning, I could see the first snows of winter just at the top of the peaks. My room had a huge open window that overlooked the fjord – there was a little beach, and then the fjord. For an hour, I watched as the sun first lit up the tops of the snow-covered mountains, then slowly crept down the valley, changing colours all the time until eventually the whole fjord was lit up. It was a fantastic show. It cost me $240 for the night, but it was well worth it. The view from the hotel window was absolutely fantastic. When I got the train back later in the morning, it was snowing in the valley for the first time that year. It was 7 October 1987.

Back at Bergen, from the mountain top to the sea, I took the overnight North Sea ferry across to the United Kingdom; a most disastrous voyage. I was seasick. I drank a little bit more than I should have that night and I was stuck in a North Sea storm. It was a very rough crossing. I was very glad I had a cabin to myself.

When I arrived at Newcastle on Tyne, I took the train first to London and then to Reading where my sister Lynnette, who I hadn't seen for more than ten years, was living. Rob, who had flown in from Greece, joined us there. Lynnette was very happy to see us both. We purloined her car for about two weeks, and drove all around southern England to beautiful places like Tintagel, Clovelly and Barnstaple, as well as Bath. Lynnette encouraged us also to do a spontaneous budget-priced trip to Paris for a few days. We saw all the usual wonders, including Versailles, and were intrigued to experience the ultimate six-lane roundabout around the Arc de Triomphe at peak hour, which put our recent circuits of all the little English roundabouts into perspective.

We returned to London for more sightseeing. Lynnette took us to Oxford and showed us the university, then we went on to Windsor, Eton and looked around Reading, of course. We flew out of London back to Australia via Athens, where we spent a few days with friends. Our flight home was with Olympic Airways – our first and last flight with that airline, and it was the last time we ever travelled in economy!

Travel really has been my all-time favourite activity. We have done so many major and minor trips together. The next big international ones with Rob included Hong Kong and Thailand in 1993, Fiji in 1995, another around the world trip in 1998, New Zealand in 2001, plus the four Captain's Choice trips. There have been too many trips, both here and overseas, to mention but I have included a list of the 67 countries I have visited by year which shows the extent of my love of international travel.

My third around the world trip with Rob in 1998 deserves a particular mention. We started predictably with a train trip, the Eastern & Oriental Express from Singapore through Thailand to Bangkok. We then flew to Italy and toured the big cities; Rome, Florence, Pisa, Genoa, Milan and more. Next we caught the Orient Express train from Venice through Innsbruck, Zurich and on to Paris. We took the ferry to Falmouth and the 'Brighton Bell' train to London and visited Lynette again in Reading. Combining car and train travel, we toured Wales and England for two weeks then flew to San Francisco, Honolulu and eventually came home through Sydney.

Countries visited by Cliff, 1968 to 2013:

Country	Year	Country	Year
Austria	1968, 1998	Bahamas	1968
Belgium	1968	Brazil	2004
Brunei	2009	Botswana	2013
Canada	1968	Chile	2004
China	1987, 2009	Croatia	1968 (then Yugoslavia)
Cuba	2004	Denmark	1968
England	1968, 1987, 1998, 2003	Fiji	1968, 1995
Finland	1987	France	1968, 1987, 1998
Germany	1968	Gibraltar	1968
Greece	1968, 1987	Hong Kong	1983, 1987, 1993, 1994, 2003, 2009
India	2011	Indonesia	1976
Ireland	1968	Italy	1968, 1998
Japan	1983, 2009	Kazakhstan	2003
Kyrgyzstan	2003	Liechtenstein	1968, 1998
Luxembourg	1968	Macedonia	1968 (then Yugoslavia)
Macau	1993, 1994	Malaysia	1975, 1976, 1994, 1998, 2009
Mexico	1968, 2004	Micronesia	2009
Monaco	1968, 2004	Mongolia	2004
Netherlands	1968	New Zealand	1968, 1976, 1977, 2001
Northern Ireland	1968	Northern Mariana Islands	2009
Norway	1987	Panama	1968
Papua New Guinea	2009	Peru	2004
Philippines	1983	Portugal	1968
Qatar	2013	Russia	1987, 2003

Country	Year	Country	Year
San Marino	1968	Scotland	1968
Serbia	1968 (then Yugoslavia)	Singapore	1975, 1987, 1998, 2003
Slovenia	1968 (then Yugoslavia)	South Africa	1968, 2013
Spain	1968	Sweden	1987
Switzerland	1968, 1998	Tanzania	2013
Thailand	1993, 1998	Turkmenistan	2003
United States of America	1968, 1998, 2009 (Guam)	Uzbekistan	2003
Vanuatu	2012	Vatican City	1968, 1998
Wales	1968, 1998	Zambia	2013
Zimbabwe	2013		

Cliff beside the Orient Express, Innsbruck, Austria, September 1998

Captain's choice tours

We then really stepped up a gear and found we were very happy to have our tours professionally organised for us by Captain's Choice, a luxury Australian tour company that we found were just the best. These tours have been excellent and, while expensive, I might add that you pay for what you get.

In 2003, we took our first of four Captain's Choice tours though China, Central Asia and Russia. This one included a train trip across China from Beijing, Xian, to Urumqi and Dzungaria Gate. We then caught a special Russian train through to Kyrgyzstan, Uzbekistan, a few other stans including Kazakhstan. Still by train, we went on to Moscow, then to St Petersburg, London, Singapore and home.

Next, in 2004, we went to Central and South America. We flew to Mexico, landing in Merida, flew to Havana in Cuba, and toured the Amazon rainforest. Our next stops were Rio de Janeiro in Brazil, and Lima and Cusco in Peru. We bussed, trained and flew across the country, ending with a tour of Easter Island on the way home.

In 2011 we travelled right across India by private train on the Maharajas' Express. It went from Mumbai through to Delhi, Agra, Bhagalpur and Shiliburi where we changed trains and took the Darjeeling Himalayan Railway to Kolkata. We flew back to Thailand and home to Melbourne. A magical trip.

The last big trip we organised was in 2013, a train trip through East Africa. We went by Rovos Rail from Tanzania to Cape Town. We went through Zambia, Zimbabwe where we saw the Victoria Falls, Botswana, took a 4WD tour through the Madikwe Game Reserve in South Africa, and spent some time in Cape Town and Johannesburg on the way home. Another magical trip.

Circumnavigating australia and new zealand

We have also travelled and are still travelling extensively in Australia, in fact to every state and territory, and especially around Victoria, multiple times. We have been to all the capital cities, including Darwin and Canberra, and most regions including the Kimberley, Kangaroo Island and Murray River, King Island, and we have crossed the Nullarbor to Kalgoorlie and Perth – all by train or car and occasionally by plane. Adding up all my road trips in the various long-suffering manual Renaults, Toyotas and Hondas, I reckon I have been around Australia a least three times. On one trip alone, I clocked up 17 000 kilometres.

The Taieri Express near Parera, South Island, New Zealand, October 2001

I have been to New Zealand four times, and twice I toured the two islands with Rob; once by car and once by coach and rail.

We have also cruised around Australia on the *Sun Princess*, explored the Kimberley on the *Coral Princess*, and sailed across the western Pacific Ocean as far as Korea and Japan and to Guam in the USA, and home via Papua New Guinea, Brisbane and Sydney on the *Dawn Princess*. Overall, we still prefer trains to ships and where necessary I am also happy to fly. My latest thrill was a surprise Qantas

747/400 flight over Antarctica on 15 February 2015 which Rob gave me for my birthday. Sadly, Rob couldn't come with me as he was in hospital with severe spinal problems. Of course, we have a plan for 2016 already; we are taking two of Australia's 'best' rail journeys on the Gulflander and the Savannahlander in North Queensland.

Cliff and Rob on the Dawn Princess, April 2009

Chapter Eleven

Reflections

After eighty years on this planet, I am allowed to reflect on what has happened since I appeared in the inglorious reign of Edward VIII in 1936.

From the first time I appreciated the news I read in newspapers and heard on radio, my earliest recollection was one of conflict. It began for me with the Second World War: the Nazis and Fascists of Europe and – of more concern to us in Australia – the militant Shintoism of the Japanese generals and the expansion of the Japanese Empire.

After these fires of ideology were extinguished, the following decades saw the military forces of Communism clashing with the 'free' world in Korea and then Vietnam. Both conflicts ended in partial defeat for both sides in Korea and total defeat for the United States and its allies in Vietnam.

The latest conflicts have flared up in the Middle East which has been a battle zone for the past four thousand years since the Egyptians took on the Canaanites before Moses. Will it ever end? Probably not; as humans we are only egos and those with 'God on their side' strive for domination of the species.

This brings me to religion and how my attitude has changed since being a Sunday school teacher in the 1940s and 50s. Reflecting on what I have read, heard and seen, I have concluded there is no supreme being, God or whatever you like to call it. It is an act of faith inspired, I suggest, by the same type of people who have led us into the conflicts – those who want to direct and shape your life and satisfy their beliefs and idealistic cravings. As I have told my friends, if there was a God he would have got rid of the human race thousands of years ago as a bad experiment. So much for religion.

Now I will come down from my 'soapbox' and reflect on the amazing changes in the area I have worked in since the 1960s, journalism. The basic approach has not changed in the job of telling people freely and accurately what is happening. Here in Australia we have restrictions, but not too many, in relating the facts. In the dictatorships and some countries verging on democracy it is a different story. The big change in the last fifty or so years has been the way the news is disseminated.

When I started, television was just beginning in the big cities. The news came mainly from the newspapers with a few radio stations providing an independent service. This relied on journalists using handwritten notes and telephones. The stories could take literally days to appear depending on the reporter's location. Then came the technical revolution: computers, mobile phones with cameras, satellite communications, instant news. I am a little envious, thinking of how we impatiently waited for film to arrive from the other side of the world, or even from the other side of Melbourne, to nowadays where someone with a camera and a mobile phone can send via satellite pictures and news of events happening in real time. It means journalists must be very well informed when making editorial decisions, there is no room for error, no time to think about it. It is a great way to get news across but a heavy responsibility on the journalist to get it right. One very good advantage is that politicians and dictators can't interfere as much; the technology helps to remove political censorship.

Finally I would like to reflect on my own life. It has been a good one, a fortunate one, and one I have enjoyed. Occasionally events didn't go as planned but generally I have been lucky, not to mention having been in the right place at the right time. When Rob and I first met, our relationship was illegal. Homosexuality was not then discussed; it was quietly hidden or forced into dark recesses. For a number of reasons, politically generally, homosexuals were harassed, humiliated and jailed by a seemingly homophobic police force. In the last forty years there has been a big cultural change, and it still continues. Certain groups, mainly religious ones, are fighting this change, I presume because it is lessening their power over the individual. These groups have also influenced our political leaders. However, change is here, and here to stay. My relationship with Rob, now recognised as a civil partnership, has been a happy and fulfilling one.

I have not wasted time or space on such emotions as hate, envy or trying to live in the past. Why waste your time and energy hating someone, when you can just ignore that person and let life go on? Why waste sweat or sleep wanting something someone else has that you cannot get? It probably doesn't matter, as there is something better around the corner. Just look for it! The past is history; let it stay that way. Learn from it by all means but don't live with it.

It has been a luxury to tell my life story and to relive it in the process of producing this biography. I have come to realise that, if there was one word to sum it all up, this word would be curiosity. Why did this or that happen? Is there a better way to achieve a better outcome? What is over the horizon?

I recall a little gravel road that turned off the Princes Highway in the Stony Rises just west of Colac in southern Victoria. The way the little road twisted out of sight behind the hills of rocks after a few metres aroused my curiosity. The first time I saw it, I was just a lad and Dad was driving. I saw it several times over the years, and was always curious about where it went. Eventually, driving on my own, I turned off the highway onto this little gravel road. After a kilometre or so, it ended at the front gate of a farm. There was nothing special about it, but my curiosity had been satisfied.

This characteristic, I am sure, is what drove me, especially in journalism, to being one of the first to hear or see the news. In travel, metaphorically speaking, I climbed to the top of the hill to see what was on the other side. Even now, with the physical limitations of old age, I still have that urge to keep exploring even if it is limited to the screen of a computer or the windows of a train or bus.

Both Rob and I expect to continue to live life to the fullest as we age gently and, using a television term, 'fade to black'.

www.ingramcontent.com/pod-product-compliance
Lightning Source LLC
Chambersburg PA
CBHW071922290426
44110CB00013B/1449